AF559995

HANDBOOK OF ANTS

HANDBOOK OF ANTS

By

Manju Yadav

Lecturer

Department of Zoology

M.M.H. College

Ghaziabad (U.P.)

(India)

DISCOVERY PUBLISHING HOUSE PVT. LTD.

NEW DELHI-110 002

Published by:
Tilak Wasan

DISCOVERY PUBLISHING HOUSE PVT. LTD.
4383/4B, Ansari Road, Darya Ganj
New Delhi-110 002 (India)
Phone : +91-11-23279245, 43596064-65
Fax : +91-11-23253475
E-mail : discoverypublishinghouse@gmail.com
sales@discoverypublishinggroup.com
parul.wasan@gmail.com
web : www.discoverypublishinggroup.com

First Edition: **2014**

ISBN: 978-93-5056-400-4

Handbook of Ants

Printed at:
Dynamic Printers
Delhi

Preface

Ants are social insects of the family **Formicidae** and, along with the related wasps and bees, belong to the order Hymenoptera. Ants evolved from wasp-like ancestors in the mid-Cretaceous period between 110 and 130 million years ago and diversified after the rise of flowering plants. More than 12,500 out of an estimated total of 22,000 species have been classified. They are easily identified by their elbowed antennae and a distinctive node-like structure that forms a slender waist. Ants form colonies that range in size from a few dozen predatory individuals living in small natural cavities to highly organised colonies that may occupy large territories and consist of millions of individuals.

Ants thrive in most ecosystems and may form 15–25% of the terrestrial animal biomass. Their success in so many environments has been attributed to their social organisation and their ability to modify habitats, tap resources, and defend themselves. Their long co-evolution with other species has led to mimetic, commensal, parasitic, and mutualistic relationships.

Ant societies have division of labour, communication between individuals, and an ability to solve complex problems. These parallels with human societies have long been an inspiration and subject of study. Many human cultures make use of ants in cuisine, medication, and rituals. Some species are valued in their role as biological pest control agents. Their ability to exploit resources may bring ants into conflict with humans, however, as they can damage crops and invade buildings. Some species, such as the red imported fire ant, are regarded as invasive species, establishing themselves in areas where they have been introduced accidentally.

A large number of text-books has also been consulted and indebeted to their writers is hereby acknowledged.

The scientific classification, life cycle, habitat, management etc. are given in this book. This book may not only provide reference but also serve as a guide and inspiration for future research. The scientists, teachers, entomologists, scholars are expected to find this book indispensable.

Author

Contents

1

Introduction

Ants are social insects of the family **Formicidae** and, along with the related wasps and bees, belong to the order Hymenoptera. Ants evolved from wasp-like ancestors in the mid-Cretaceous period between 110 and 130 million years ago and diversified after the rise of flowering plants. More than 12,500 out of an estimated total of 22,000 species have been classified. They are easily identified by their elbowed antennae and a distinctive node-like structure that forms a slender waist. Ants form colonies that range in size from a few dozen predatory individuals living in small natural cavities to highly organised colonies that may occupy large territories and consist of millions of individuals.

Larger colonies consist mostly of sterile wingless females forming castes of "workers", "soldiers", or other specialised groups. Nearly all ant colonies also have some fertile males called "drones" and one or more fertile females called "queens". The colonies sometimes are described as superorganisms because the ants appear to operate as a unified entity, collectively working together to support the colony. Ants have colonised almost every landmass on Earth. The only places lacking indigenous ants are Antarctica and a few remote or inhospitable islands.

Ants thrive in most ecosystems and may form 15–25% of the terrestrial animal biomass. Their success in so many environments has been attributed to their social organisation and their ability to modify habitats, tap resources, and defend themselves. Their long co-evolution with other species has led to mimetic, commensal, parasitic, and mutualistic relationships.

Ant societies have division of labour, communication between individuals, and an ability to solve complex problems. These parallels with human societies have long been an inspiration and subject of study. Many human cultures make use of ants in cuisine, medication, and rituals. Some species are valued in their role as biological pest control agents. Their ability to exploit resources may bring ants into conflict with humans, however, as they can damage crops and invade buildings. Some species, such as the red imported fire ant, are regarded as invasive species, establishing themselves in areas where they have been introduced accidentally.

Etymology

The word *ant* is derived from *ante* of Middle English which is derived from *æmette* of Old English and is related to the Old High German *âmeiza*, hence the modern German *Ameise*. All of these words come from West Germanic **amaitjo*, and the original meaning of the word was "the biter" (from Proto-Germanic **ai-*, "off, away" + **mait-* "cut"). The family name *Formicidae* is derived from the Latin *formîca* ("ant") from which the words in other Romance languages such as the Portuguese *formiga*, Italian *formica*, Spanish *hormiga*, Romanian *furnică* and French *fourmi* are derived. It has been hypothetized that a Proto-Indo-European word *morwi- was used, cf. Sanskrit vamrah, Latin formîca, Greek myrmex, Old Church Slavonic mraviji, Old Irish moirb, Old Norse maurr.

Taxonomy and Evolution

The family Formicidae belongs to the order Hymenoptera, which also includes sawflies, bees, and wasps. Ants evolved from a lineage within the vespoid wasps. Fossil evidence indicates that ants were present in the Late Jurassic, 150 million years ago. After the rise of flowering plants about 100 million years ago they diversified and assumed ecological dominance around 60 million years ago. Researchers identified the fossil remains of an ant (*Sphecomyrma freyi*) that lived in the Cretaceous period. The specimen, trapped in amber dating back to more than 80 million years ago, has features of both ants and wasps. *Sphecomyrma* probably was a ground forager, but some suggest on the basis of groups such as the Leptanillinae and Martialinae, that primitive ants were likely to have been predators underneath the surface of the soil.

During the Cretaceous period, a few species of primitive ants ranged widely on the Laurasian super-continent (the northern hemisphere). They were scarce in comparison to the populations of other insects, representing only approximately 1% of the entire insect population. Ants became dominant after adaptive radiation at the beginning of the Paleogene period. By the Oligocene and Miocene ants had come to represent 20–40% of all insects found in major fossil deposits. Of the species that lived in the Eocene epoch, approximately one in ten genera survive to the present.

Genera surviving today comprise 56% of the genera in Baltic amber fossils (early Oligocene), and 92% of the genera in Dominican amber fossils (apparently early Miocene).

Termites, although sometimes called *white ants*, are not ants. They belong to the order Isoptera. Termites are more closely related to cockroaches and mantids. Termites are eusocial, but differ greatly in the genetics of reproduction. That their social structure is similar to that of ants, is attributed to convergent evolution. Velvet ants look like large ants, but are wingless female wasps.

Ants are found on all continents except Antarctica, and only a few large islands such as Greenland, Iceland, parts of Polynesia and the Hawaiian Islands lack native ant species. Ants occupy a wide range of ecological niches, and are able to exploit a wide range of food resources either as direct or indirect herbivores, predators, and scavengers. Most species are omnivorous generalists, but a few are specialist feeders. Their ecological dominance may be measured by their biomass and estimates in different environments suggest that they contribute 15–20% (on average and nearly 25% in the tropics) of the total terrestrial animal biomass, which exceeds that of the vertebrates.

Distribution and Diversity

Region	No. of species
Neotropics	2162
Nearctic	580
Europe	180
Africa	2500
Asia	2080
Melanesia	275
Australia	985
Polynesia	42

Ants range in size from 0.75 to 52 millimetres (0.030–2.0 in), the largest species being the fossil *Titanomyrma giganteum*, the queen of which was 6 centimetres (2.4 in) long with a wingspan of 15 centimetres (5.9 in). Ants vary in colour; most ants are red or black, but a few species are green and some tropical species have a metallic lustre. More than 12,000 species are currently known (with upper estimates of the potential existence of about 22,000), with the greatest diversity in the tropics. Taxonomic studies continue to resolve the classification and systematics of ants. Online databases of ant species, including AntBase and the Hymenoptera Name Server, help to keep track of the known and newly described species. The relative ease with which ants may be sampled and studied in ecosystems has made them useful as indicator species in biodiversity studies.

Bull ant showing the powerful mandibles and the relatively large compound eyes that provide excellent vision

MORPHOLOGY

Ants are distinct in their morphology from other insects in having elbowed antennae, metapleural glands, and a strong constriction of their second abdominal segment into a node-like petiole. The head, mesosoma, and metasoma are the three distinct body segments. The petiole forms a narrow waist between their mesosoma (thorax plus the first abdominal segment, which is fused to it) and gaster (abdomen less the abdominal segments in the petiole). The petiole may be formed by one or two nodes (the second alone, or the second and third abdominal segments).

Like other insects, ants have an exoskeleton, an external covering that provides a protective casing around the body and a point of attachment for muscles, in contrast to the internal skeletons of humans and other vertebrates. Insects do not have lungs; oxygen and other gases such as carbon dioxide pass through their exoskeleton via tiny valves called spiracles. Insects also lack closed blood vessels; instead, they have a long, thin, perforated tube along the top of the body (called the "dorsal aorta") that functions like a heart, and pumps haemolymph toward the head, thus driving the circulation of the internal fluids. The nervous system consists of a ventral

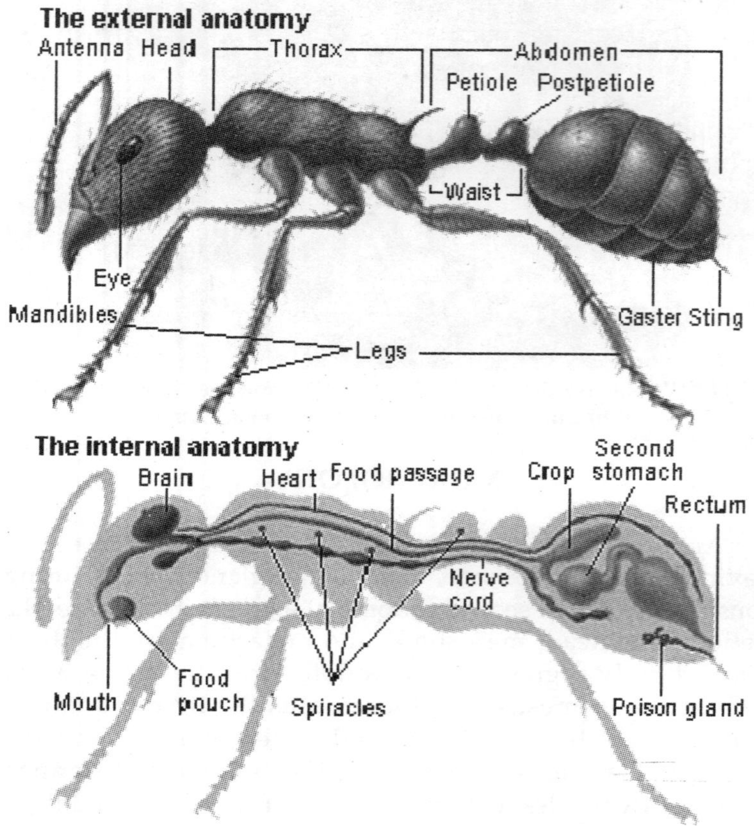

Diagram of ant : External and Internal Anatomy

nerve cord that runs the length of the body, with several ganglia and branches along the way reaching into the extremities of the appendages.Diagram of a worker ant (*Pachycondyla verenae*)

Head

An ant's head contains many sensory organs. Like most insects, ants have compound eyes made from numerous tiny lenses attached together. Ant eyes are good for acute movement detection, but do not offer a high resolution image. They also have three small ocelli (simple eyes) on the top of the head that detect light levels and polarization. Compared to vertebrates, most ants have poor-to-mediocre eyesight and a few subterranean species are completely blind. Some ants such as Australia's bulldog ant, however, have excellent vision and are capable of discriminating the distance and size of objects moving nearly a metre away.

Two antennae ("feelers") are attached to the head; these organs detect chemicals, air currents, and vibrations; they also are used to transmit and receive signals through touch. The head has two strong jaws, the mandibles, used to carry food, manipulate objects, construct nests, and for defence. In some species a small pocket (infrabuccal chamber) inside the mouth stores food, so it may be passed to other ants or their larvae.

Legs

All six legs are attached to the mesosoma ("thorax"). A hooked claw at the end of each leg helps ants to climb and to hang onto surfaces.

Wings

Most queens and the small number of drones in a colony (the male ants), have wings; queens shed the wings after the nuptial fli t, leaving visible stubs, a distinguishing feature of queens. Wingless queens (ergatoids) and males occur in a few species, however.

Metasoma

The metasoma (the "abdomen") of the ant houses important internal organs, including those of the reproductive, respiratory (tracheae), and excretory systems. Workers of many species have their egg-laying structures modified into stings that are used for subduing prey and defending their nests.

Polymorphism

In the colonies of a few ant species, there are physical castes—workers in distinct size-classes, called minor, median, and major workers. Often the larger ants have disproportionately larger heads, and correspondingly stronger mandibles. Such individuals sometimes are called "soldier" ants because their stronger mandibles make them more effective in fighting, although they still are workers and their "duties" typically do not vary greatly from the minor or median workers.

In a few species the median workers are absent, creating a sharp divide between the minors and majors. Weaver ants, for example, have a distinct bimodal size distribution. Some other species show continuous variation in the size of workers. The smallest and largest workers in Pheidologeton diversus show nearly a 500-fold difference in their dry-weights. Workers cannot mate; however, because of the haplodiploid sex-determination system in ants, workers of a number of species can lay unfertilised eggs that become fully fertile, haploid males. The role of workers may change with their age and in some species, such as honeypot ants, young workers are fed until their gasters are distended, and act as living food storage vessels.

These food storage workers are called *repletes*. This polymorphism in morphology and behaviour of workers initially was thought to be determined by environmental factors such as nutrition and hormones that led to different developmental paths; however, genetic differences between worker castes have been noted in *Acromyrmex* sp.

These polymorphisms are caused by relatively small genetic changes; differences in a single gene of *Solenopsis invicta* can decide whether the colony will have single or multiple queens. The Australian jack jumper ant (*Myrmecia pilosula*) has only a single pair of chromosomes (with the males having just one chromosome as they are haploid), the lowest number known for any animal, making it an interesting subject for studies in the genetics and developmental biology of social insects.

DESCRIPTION

Body

Ants vary in length from about 1/16 inch (1.6 mm) to nearly 2 inches (5 cm). Most species are red, black, brown, or yellow, and some are green or metallic blue. Ants, like other insects, have six legs. Their bodies are divided into three distinct segments: head, thorax, and abdomen. Unlike other insects, ants have elbowed (rather than straight or curved) antennae (feelers), and a pedicel, a narrow waistlike indentation between the thorax and abdomen. The crop, an organ located in the abdomen, is used to store food, which can later be regurgitated to feed other members of the colony.

Most ants are smooth-bodied, although some have spiny projections. Ants have strong jaws called mandibles, which are adapted for killing, crushing, chewing, cutting, or tearing, depending on the species and what it eats. Some species of ants have glands that produce formic acid, a strong acid that can be squirted on enemies, causing a burn or sting. Many ants have stingers that contain poison, and some, such as the harvester ants and fire ants, can inflict painful and, occasionally, fatal stings on humans and other animals.

Why Do Ants Have Tiny Waists?

Ants have tiny waists so they can wriggle their end parts freely! An ant's waist has one or two movable parts. These parts allow the ant to twist and turn in different ways—an important feature for moving about an ant colony.

Ants have three main body parts: the head, the trunk, and the metasoma. The ant's eyes, antennae, and mandibles are located on its head.

Attached to the trunk are six legs with segments. Each leg has two claws at the foot. The claws hook into dirt, tree bark, or leaves, so ants can quickly walk, climb, and dig! Ants are strong, too. Many ants can lift 50 times their body weight!

The metasoma has two parts. They are the waist and the gaster. Organs for digesting, getting rid of waste, and reproducing are in the gaster. Some ant species have a sting at the end of the gaster to defend against other insects.

Where Do Ants Live?

There are about 10,000 species of ants. So it is not surprising that ants, like millions of other social insects, live everywhere on land, except where it is really cold. In fact, areas with warm and moist climates have the most types of ants and other insects.

Tropical rain forests are very rich in insect life. If all the animals in the Amazon rain forest were weighed, many scientists think ants and termites would make up one-third of that weight.

Ants are successful survivors. They have different ways of life that allow them to live in different habitats. And their small size makes it easy for them to find food and shelter.

Senses

The ant's most highly developed sense is that of smell. Ants have abdominal glands that secrete a variety of pheromones, chemical substances that cause specific reactions by other individuals. Pheromones act as alarms, sex attractants, and trail markers; and they help individuals recognize each other. Ants have a well-developed sense of taste, and can distinguish sour, sweet, bitter, and salty tastes. Their sense of touch is keen. Touch, or tactile, receptors are located on the feet and on hairs on the legs. The antennae are used for smelling, tasting, and touching.

Some species of ants have compound eyes and well-developed vision, while others have simple eyes that can only distinguish between light and dark. Some species of ants are blind.

Habits

Homes

Ants typically make their nests in or on the ground. The soil excavated to make the nest may be piled up around the opening to the nest, forming a mound or crater. The nest is typically composed of several long tunnels that lead to chambers. The chambers serve as storage areas for food and as nurseries for the young.

Some ants live in the wood of trees or rotten logs. The workers of one tree-dwelling species make nests by weaving leaves together with silky threads secreted by their larvae. Some ants have well-defined territories and build permanent nests. Others move from one site to another, building a new nest each time. Some ants share their nests with ants of a different species and sometimes with other kinds of insects, or with spiders. A number of ants make their nests in human dwellings, particularly in wood siding or in the foundation.

Food

Some species of ants eat live insects while others feed only on decaying animal matter. Others cultivate and eat fungi. Some ants gather seeds and grain for food. Several ant species tend "herds" of aphids and scale insects to obtain the sugary liquid, called honeydew, that they excrete.

WHAT ELSE DO ANTS EAT?

Ants eat fruit, flowers, and seeds, while others eat everything in their path, including small animals.

Ants have special mouthparts for grabbing and eating food. First come the mandibles, which are jaws that move from side to side. Ants use their mandibles to hold food, carry their young, and fight enemies. Behind the mandibles are the maxillae (mak SIHL ee), which are used for chewing. But ants do not swallow the food right away. First the food passes to a pouch behind the mouth. There, the liquid is squeezed out of the food. Ants swallow the liquid and spit out the leftover food pellet.

Ants have two kinds of stomachs—a stomach and a crop. Food an ant eats for itself goes to the stomach. Food it shares with others is stored in the crop. The ant spits up this food to feed other ants and larvae. Hungry ants may stroke each other or tap antennae to ask for food.

The Ant Colony

Ants are social insects, living in large colonies. The colony is typically divided into the following castes, or classes: queens (reproductive females), males, and workers (nonreproductive females). Although there are great variations in social structure among ant colonies, certain basic features are common to most species. These features are described in the following section.

What is a Social Insect?

Ants, termites, many bees, and some wasps have a real family life. They live in communities, and the members of a community depend on one another.

There are more than a million different species, or kinds, of insects in the world. Insects include beetles, crickets, butterflies, and houseflies. Insects come in many different shapes, sizes, and colors. But there are some things that all insects have in common. They all have six legs and bodies that are divided into three main parts. They all have tough, shell-like body coverings. And most, but not all, have wings.

Ants, termites, bees, and wasps may look a lot like these other insects. But as social insects, they lead very different lives.

Why Are Ants Social Insects?

Ants are social insects because they live and work together in communities. Here, they feed and protect one another. They raise and care for their young. This way of life is very different from that of solitary insects that spend most, and sometimes all, of their lives alone.

An ant community is called a colony (KAHL uh nee). Life in an ant colony is very organized. Each member has a job to do, from laying eggs to gathering food to fighting.

For most ants, colony life centers around the nest. The nest may be underground, in a mound, or even among the treetops. When ants build a nest, the dirt that piles up around the entrance forms an anthill.An ant colony is a very busy place. It can also be very crowded. There may be hundreds, thousands, or even millions of ants in a single colony.

Social Castes

Some colonies have one queen; other colonies have several. The queens are fed and otherwise tended by the workers. The males' only function is to mate with the queens.

The workers carry out such tasks as enlarging and protecting the nest, tending queens and young, and foraging. There may be only one kind of worker, or there may be several kinds, with body structures specialized for different types of work. The activity of workers is coordinated mostly through pheromones and body contact.

Depending on the species, queens live about 5 to 30 years, making them the longest-lived insects. Workers live about 1 to 3 years. Males live only for a mating season.

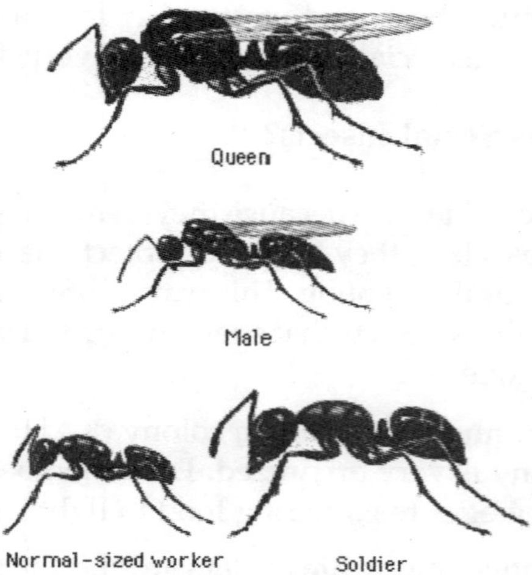

Ants have complex social organization and specialized castes.

Who's Who in an Ant Colony?

Like most social insects, ants have three castes, or classes. There are queen ants, worker ants, and male ants.A queen does not rule the colony, but she is an important member. She has one job—to lay eggs. Without her, a colony would die out. The reason is that only the queens in most species of ants can reproduce. They also live the longest—10 to 20 years. A colony may have one or more queens. A European wood ant mound, for example, may have hundreds of queens.

Worker ants may be the smallest, but they do the most work. All the workers are females. They care for the queen and her young. Worker ants build and repair the nest. They search for food and fight off enemies. Worker ants usually live one to five years.

Most male ants live only a few weeks or months. They do not work, and they die shortly after mating with young queens.

What Does an Ant Nest Look Like?

Most ant species build underground nests. Worker ants dig tunnels and chambers, or rooms, in the soil. As the colony grows, workers add more tunnels and chambers to the nest.

Ant colonies can grow to be quite large. Some tropical ants build downward to make more room. Their nests may reach 20 feet (6 meters) below the ground. Others, such as European wood ants, build upward. They build huge mound nests that may be 5 feet (1.5 meters) tall. Then the ants connect the mounds with scent trails. The group of nests may cover an area as large as a tennis court. Millions of ants may live in these nests.

The chambers in an ant nest have many different uses. The queen has her own chamber for laying eggs. Some chambers are nurseries for the growing young. Food is stored in other chambers. Still other chambers are resting places for hard-working ants!

Starting A Colony

Usually once a year, a colony produces a generation of queens and males. Queens develop from larvae fed a highly nutritious substance secreted by workers. Males develop from unfertilized eggs.

The queens and males are winged; they leave the nest in a series of large swarms, known as nuptial flights. Each swarm consists of either all queens or all males. The ants fly to other areas to mate with ants from other colonies. The males die after the flight. The queens drop to the ground, shed their wings, and look for a place to lay their eggs. After a single mating, a queen can lay fertilized eggs for several years. Unfertilized eggs are usually laid sometime in the spring or summer. The eggs develop into larvae, the larvae into pupae, and the pupae into adults—a process called complete metamorphosis.

The queen tends her first brood of offspring during their larval and pupal stages. This generation consists only of workers, who then take over the duties of tending the queen and her subsequent broods.

How Does a Queen Ant Start a Colony?

Most species of ants start a new colony in the same way. A queen ant is born in one colony, but she usually leaves that colony to start a new one. As young queens grow, they develop wings. A few weeks after becoming adults, young queens fly out of the nest to mate with winged males. The queens then shed their wings and look for nesting places.

When a young queen finds a nesting spot, she builds a chamber and seals herself inside. Then she begins to lay eggs. The queen cares for the eggs, which develop into larvae (lahr vee) and then pupae (PYOO pee). The queen feeds the young with her saliva. She does not eat during this time. Her body absorbs the unneeded wing muscles as food.

The eggs develop into small, female worker ants. Some of these workers leave the nest to find food for the colony. Others build onto the nest. The queen lays more eggs. Most develop into female workers. Others develop into males and young queens.

What Do Worker Ants Do?

Worker ants work¾and they work hard. All workers are females. But they very rarely become queens or reproduce. Instead, they care for the queen, the young ants, and the nest. Without its workers, an ant colony could not survive.

Worker ants may have one job or several jobs. They may keep the same job all their lives or change jobs from time to time. Some workers gather food for the colony. They store the food they harvest in special chambers in the nest. Other workers feed and care for the queen and her developing young. Still others build the chambers and tunnels. They use their saliva to make the dirt walls hard.

Some worker ants are soldiers. They defend the colony. In many species, soldier ants are larger than the other workers. The soldiers fight off enemy ants or insects. They may also use their large heads to block the entrances to the nest.

Who Is Minding the Eggs?

Ants go through four different stages, or steps, of growth. These stages are egg, larva, pupa, and adult. Worker ants care for the young ants through each stage.

After a queen ant lays her eggs, worker ants take them to hatching chambers. There, the workers care for the eggs and often groom them by licking. The eggs hatch in a few days to become larvae. During the larvae stage, the young ants look like tiny white worms.

Worker ants move the larvae to new chambers and feed them for a few weeks until they become pupae. In some species, the larvae spin cocoons before they become pupae. In other species, the pupae are covered only by thin, see-through skin. Pupae do not eat or move. But they do change. In two to three weeks, adult ants come out of the cocoons or skin. They are now ready to go to work!

How Do Ants Recognize Each Other?

Ants in a colony have a special odor that helps them recognize one another. Outsiders or enemies have different odors. Soldier ants smell these invaders and kill them.

Ants do not have ears. They "hear" vibrations through their sense organs. An ant's antennae are its most important sense organ. Ants use their antennae to smell, touch, taste, and hear. It's easy to see why an ant's antennae are always moving. Antennae help ants find and taste food. They help ants recognize and touch one another. Antennae even help ants find their way.

Most ants have two compound eyes. A compound eye has many lenses. (A human eye has only one lens.) Because of their compound lenses, ants see things broken up, like an image in a kaleidoscope. Ants see movement better than shape.

KINDS OF ANTS

There are about 10,000 species of ants. Many species are familiar to humans, although many others are seldom seen, living almost entirely underground, or foraging only at night. Among the interesting or unusual ants are the following:

Carpenter Ants

Carpenter ants build nests and tunnels in dead wood, trees, utility poles, and timbers of buildings. Although they do not eat the wood, carpenter ants can do considerable damage to it. Carpenter ants are found in temperate regions throughout the world. The workers are among the largest known ants. The black carpenter ant is the largest ant found in the United States. The workers are about half an inch (1.3 cm) long, and the queens about one inch (2.5 cm). This ant sometimes enters houses in search of sweet foods.

Driver, or Army, Ants

Driver, or Army, Ants move their entire colonies every two to four weeks. They are found mainly in Africa and tropical America. Several species are found in the southern and southwestern United States, where they are called legionary ants. Driver ants are predatory, and their foraging parties are noted for ridding large areas of insects, lizards, and other small animals. Their sting is very poisonous, and they have been known to kill chickens and some larger animals. Driver ants have several kinds of workers, including soldiers. The soldiers are larger than other workers and have strong, hooked jaws.

Driver ants are nomadic; their movements are related to the hatching and growth of successive broods. While eggs are being laid and are hatching into larvae, the colony stays in one place. During this time, a previous generation hatches from pupae into adults. The entire colony then moves on to the next site through a leaf-covered tunnel built by the workers. The larvae are carried to the new site in the mouths of some of the workers.

Which Ants Are on the Move?

Army ants—thousands to millions of them—are almost always on the move. They do not build permanent nests. They just march along, carrying their young and looking for food. They kill and eat anything in their path. This usually includes spiders and other insects. But in some cases, army ants prey on larger animals that cannot get away quickly.

Each night, army ants stop to rest. They gather together to form a cluster on a tree branch or in a log. The queen and the developing ants rest deep within the cluster, where they will be safe.

When the queen is laying eggs, the army ants cluster in the same spot each night. They remain at this temporary campsite until all the eggs have developed into active larvae. When the larvae begin to grow, the cluster moves to a new spot each evening.

Fire Ants

Fire Ants are native to South America but are now also found in the southern United States. They eat a variety of foods, including fruit, vegetables, and insects. Fire ants are named for their painful sting, which produces a burning sensation. Armies of fire ants have been known to kill livestock. They are agricultural pests because they destroy young crop plants. Fire ants cover their nests with mounds of hard soil, some reaching a height of two feet (60 cm). They enter and exit the nest through several tunnels excavated in the mound.

Fungus-growing Ants

Fungus-growing Ants, found only in the New World, cultivate a certain species of fungus for their food. Some species of fungus-growing ants cut off leaves from trees and other plants and carry them to their nests. They chew the leaves into a pulp and use it as a base on which to grow the fungus. These ants are commonly called leaf-cutting ants. They are also called parasol ants because they hold the leaves over their heads when carrying them. Some fungus-growing ants construct their gardens from insect droppings.

Which Ants Farm Fungus?

Leaf-cutter ants are farmers that grow their own food in underground gardens. The food they grow is a fungus, a kind of mold or mildew. The ants fertilize their fungus gardens with bits of leaves.

Leaf-cutters build huge colonies. Their nests can have a thousand chambers and tunnel down 20 feet (6 meters). Inside, up to a million ants may be at work.

Big and little ants are needed to farm the fungus. Large worker ants set out at night to gather leaves. They use their long, hooked mandibles to cut the leaves. Then they march back

Leaf-cutting ants cultivate fungus for food

to the nest, holding the leaves high. For this reason, leaf-cutters are often called umbrella or parasol ants.

Inside the nest, smaller workers chew the leaves into a pulp, or paste. They put this paste on the fungus. Later, tiny ants harvest the fungus to feed the colony.

Harvester Ants

Harvester Ants gather and store certain wild grass seeds, or cultivated grain. They gather the seeds from the plants and pick up those that have fallen to the ground. They store the seeds in underground chambers, and bring them up on sunny days and spread them out to dry. There are several species of harvester ants, found in temperate and subtropical regions. They can inflict very painful bites and stings.

Honey Ants

Honey Ants use certain workers, called repletes, as living vessels in which to store food. They collect nectar from plants or honeydew exuded by other nectar-eating insects and feed it to these workers. The repletes are gorged until their abdomens are many times normal size and they cannot move about. They hang from the ceilings of nest chambers and dispense the food, by regurgitating it, to the other ants during dry seasons when other food and water are scarce. There are a number of species of honey ants. They are found in the southwestern United States, Mexico, Australia, New Guinea, and parts of Africa.

Which Ants Herd Aphids?

Dairying ants "herd" aphids (AY fihdz)—just as people herd cattle! The ants keep the aphids together and protect them from other insects. Why do the ants do this? It's because aphids produce something that the ants really like—honeydew. Aphids are small insects that suck plant juices and give off the excess as honeydew. Dairying ants eat the honeydew. They use their antennae to stroke the aphids, causing them to produce more of the sweet, sugary liquid.

Dairying ants take good care of their aphids. They will move their herd if the aphids need better plants to eat. They even store aphid eggs in their nests through the winter to start a new herd in the spring. A young queen may also take along an egg-laying aphid when she starts a new colony. This queen carries the aphid in her mandibles.

Black Ants

Little black ants are native to the United States and are found throughout most parts of the country. They are found in houses, in the cracks in sidewalks, and on lawns. Little black ants are attracted to human foods, particularly cooked meats and vegetables, and those containing sugar. They are active day and night, and are often seen carrying food back to their nests.

Slave-holding Ants

Slave-holding ants raid the nests of other ant species for larvae and pupae, which become slave workers in their colony after growing to adulthood. Some species of slave-holding ants are called amazon ants. Some slave-holding ants can live without slaves, if necessary. Other species are completely dependent, being unable to carry on the tasks of their colony alone. Slave-holding ants are widely distributed throughout the world.

DEVELOPMENT AND REPRODUCTION

The life of an ant starts from an egg. If the egg is fertilised, the progeny will be female (diploid); if not, it will be male (haploid). Ants develop by complete metamorphosis with the larva stages passing through a pupal stage before emerging as an adult. The larva is largely immobile and is fed and cared for by workers.

Food is given to the larvae by trophallaxis, a process in which an ant regurgitates liquid food held in its crop. This is also how adults share food, stored in the "social stomach". Larvae may also be provided with solid food such as trophic eggs, pieces of prey, and seeds brought back by foraging workers and the larvae may even be transported directly to captured prey in some species.

The larvae grow through a series of moults and enter the pupal stage. The pupa has the appendages free and not fused to the body as in a butterfly pupa. The differentiation into queens and workers (which are both female), and different castes of workers (when they exist), is influenced in some species by the nutrition the larvae obtain. Genetic influences and the control of gene expression by the developmental environment are complex and the determination of caste continues to be a subject of research. Larvae and pupae need to be kept at fairly constant temperatures to ensure proper development, and so often, are moved around among the various brood chambers within the colony.

A new worker spends the first few days of its adult life caring for the queen and young. She then graduates to digging and other nest work, and later to defending the nest and foraging. These changes are sometimes fairly sudden, and define what are called temporal castes. An explanation for the sequence is suggested by the high casualties involved in foraging, making it an acceptable risk only for ants who are older and are likely to die soon of natural causes.

Most ant species have a system in which only the queen and breeding females have the ability to mate. Contrary to popular belief, some ant nests have multiple queens while others may exist without queens. Workers with the ability to reproduce are called "gamergates" and colonies that lack queens are then called gamergate colonies; colonies with queens are said to be queen-right. The winged male ants, called drones, emerge from pupae along with the breeding females (although some species, such as army ants, have wingless queens), and do nothing in life except eat and mate.

Most ants are univoltine, producing a new generation each year. During the species-specific breeding period, new reproductives, females and winged males leave the colony in what is called a nuptial flight. Typically, the males take flight before the females. Males then use visual cues to find a common mating ground, for example, a landmark such as a pine tree to which other males in the area converge. Males secrete a mating pheromone that females follow. Females of some species mate with just one male, but in some others they may mate with as many as ten or more different males.

Mated females then seek a suitable place to begin a colony. There, they break off their wings and begin to lay and care for eggs. The females store the sperm they obtain during their nuptial flight to selectively fertilise future eggs. The first workers to hatch are weak and smaller than later workers, but they begin to serve the colony immediately. They enlarge the nest, forage for food, and care for the other eggs. This is how new colonies start in most ant species. Species that have multiple queens may have a queen leaving the nest along with some workers to found a colony at a new site, a process akin to swarming in honeybees.

A wide range of reproductive strategies have been noted in ant species. Females of many species are known to be capable of reproducing asexually through thelytokous parthenogenesis and one species, *Mycocepurus smithii*, is known to be all-female.

Ants mating

Ant colonies can be long-lived. The queens can live for up to 30 years, and workers live from 1 to 3 years. Males, however, are more transitory, being quite short-lived and surviving for only a few weeks. Ant queens are estimated to live 100 times longer than solitary insects of a similar size.

Ants are active all year long in the tropics, but, in cooler regions, they survive the winter in a state of dormancy or inactivity. The forms of inactivity are varied and some temperate species have larvae going into the inactive state, (diapause), while in others, the adults alone pass the winter in a state of reduced activity.

BEHAVIOUR AND ECOLOGY

Communication

Weaver ants collaborating to dismember a red ant (the two at the extremities are pulling the red ant, while the middle one cuts the red ant until it snaps).

Ants communicate with each other using pheromones, sounds, and touch. The use of pheromomes as chemical signals is more developed in ants than in other hymenopteran groups. Like other insects, ants perceive smells with their long, thin, and mobile antennae. The paired antennae provide information about the direction and intensity of scents. Since most ants live on the ground, they use the soil surface to leave pheromone trails that may be followed by other ants. In species that forage in groups, a forager that finds food marks a trail on the way back to the colony; this trail is followed by other ants, these ants then reinforce the trail when they head back with food to the colony. When the food source is exhausted, no new trails are marked by returning ants and the scent slowly dissipates. This behaviour helps ants deal with changes in their environment. For instance, when an established path to a food source is blocked by an obstacle, the foragers leave the path to explore new routes. If an ant is successful, it leaves a new trail marking the shortest route on its return. Successful trails are followed by more ants, reinforcing better routes and gradually identifying the best path.

Ants use pheromones for more than just making trails. A crushed ant emits an alarm pheromone that sends nearby ants into an attack frenzy and attracts more ants from farther away. Several ant species even use "propaganda pheromones" to confuse enemy ants and make them fight among themselves. Pheromones are produced by a wide range of structures including Dufour's glands, poison glands and glands on the hindgut, pygidium, rectum, sternum, and hind tibia. Pheromones also are exchanged, mixed with food, and passed by trophallaxis, transferring information within the colony. This allows other ants to detect what task group (*e.g.*, foraging or nest maintenance) to which other colony members belong. In ant species with queen castes, when the dominant queen stops producing a specific pheromone, workers begin to raise new queens in the colony.

Some ants produce sounds by stridulation, using the gaster segments and their mandibles. Sounds may be used to communicate with colony members or with other species.

Defence

Ants attack and defend themselves by biting and, in many species, by stinging, often injecting or spraying chemicals such as formic acid. Bullet ants (*Paraponera*), located in Central and South America, are considered to have the most painful sting of any insect, although it is usually not fatal to humans. This sting is given the highest rating on the Schmidt Sting Pain Index.

The sting of Jack jumper ants can be fatal, and an antivenom has been developed for it.

Fire ants, *Solenopsis* spp., are unique in having a poison sac containing piperidine alkaloids. Their stings are painful and can be dangerous to hypersensitive people.

Trap-jaw ants of the genus *Odontomachus* are equipped with mandibles called trap-jaws, which snap shut faster than any other predatory appendages within the animal kingdom. One study of *Odontomachus bauri* recorded peak speeds of between 126 and 230 km/h (78-143 mph), with the jaws closing within 130 microseconds on average. The ants were also observed to use their jaws as a catapult to eject intruders or fling themselves backward to escape a threat. Before striking, the ant opens its mandibles extremely widely and locks them in this position by an internal mechanism. Energy is stored in a thick band of muscle and explosively released when triggered by the stimulation of sensory organs resembling hairs on the inside of the mandibles. The mandibles also permit slow and fine movements for other tasks. Trap-jaws also are seen in the following genera: *Anochetus, Orectognathus*, and *Strumigenys*, plus some members of the Dacetini tribe, which are viewed as examples of convergent evolution.

A Malaysian species of ant in the *Camponotus cylindricus* group has enlarged mandibular glands that extend into their gaster. When disturbed, workers rupture the membrane of the gaster, causing a burst of secretions containing acetophenones and other chemicals that immobilise small insect attackers. The worker subsequently dies.

Suicidal defences by workers are also noted in a Brazilian ant, *Forelius pusillus*, where a small group of ants leaves the security of the nest after sealing the entrance from the outside each evening.

In addition to defence against predators, ants need to protect their colonies from pathogens. Some worker ants maintain the hygiene of the colony and their activities include undertaking or *necrophory*, the disposal of dead nest-mates. Oleic acid has been identified as the compound released from dead ants that triggers necrophoric behaviour in *Atta mexicana* while workers of *Linepithema humile* react to the absence of characteristic chemicals (dolichodial and iridomyrmecin) present on the cuticle of their living nestmates to trigger similar behaviour.

Nests may be protected from physical threats such as flooding and overheating by elaborate nest architecture. Workers of *Cataulacus muticus*, an arboreal species that lives in plant hollows, respond to flooding by drinking water inside the nest, and excreting it outside. *Camponotus anderseni*, which nests in the cavities of wood in mangrove habitats, deals with submergence under water by switching to anaerobic respiration.

Learning

Many animals can learn behaviours by imitation, but ants may be the only group apart from mammals where interactive teaching has been observed. A knowledgeable forager of *Temnothorax albipennis* will lead a naive nest-mate to newly discovered food by the process of tandem running. The follower obtains knowledge through its leading tutor. Both leader and follower are acutely sensitive to the progress of their partner with the leader slowing down when the follower lags, and speeding up when the follower gets too close.

Controlled experiments with colonies of *Cerapachys biroi* suggest that an individual may choose nest roles based on her previous experience. An entire generation of identical workers was divided into two groups whose outcome in food foraging was controlled. One group was continually rewarded with prey, while it was made certain that the other failed. As a result, members of the successful group intensified their foraging attempts while the unsuccessful group ventured out fewer and fewer times. A month later, the successful foragers continued in their role while the others had moved to specialise in brood care.

Nest Construction

Complex nests are built by many ant species, but other species are nomadic and do not build permanent structures. Ants may form subterranean nests or build them on trees. These nests may be found in the ground, under stones or logs, inside logs,

Leaf nest of weaver ants

hollow stems, or even acorns. The materials used for construction include soil and plant matter, and ants carefully select their nest sites; *Temnothorax albipennis* will avoid sites with dead ants, as these may indicate the presence of pests or disease. They are quick to abandon established nests at the first sign of threats.

The army ants of South America and the driver ants of Africa do not build permanent nests, but instead, alternate between nomadism and stages where the workers form a temporary nest (bivouac) from their own bodies, by holding each other together.

Weaver ant (*Oecophylla* spp.) workers build nests in trees by attaching leaves together, first pulling them together with bridges of workers and then inducing their larvae to produce silk as they are moved along the leaf edges. Similar forms of nest construction are seen in some species of *Polyrhachis*.

Some ant species build nests in and on buildings. Interior spaces in walls, windows, and even electric appliances such as clocks, lamps, and radios in the interior of buildings may be used as sites for nests.

Cultivation of Food

Most ants are generalist predators, scavengers, and indirect herbivores, but a few have evolved specialised ways of

***Myrmecocystus*, honeypot ants, store food to prevent colony famine**

obtaining nutrition. Leafcutter ants (*Atta* and *Acromyrmex*) feed exclusively on a fungus that grows only within their colonies. They continually collect leaves which are taken to the colony, cut into tiny pieces and placed in fungal gardens. Workers specialise in related tasks according to their sizes. The largest ants cut stalks, smaller workers chew the leaves and the smallest tend the fungus. Leafcutter ants are sensitive enough to recognise the reaction of the fungus to different plant material, apparently detecting chemical signals from the fungus. If a particular type of leaf is found to be toxic to the fungus, the colony will no longer collect it. The ants feed on structures produced by the fungi called, *gongylidia*. Symbiotic bacteria on the exterior surface of the ants produce antibiotics that kill bacteria introduced into the nest that may harm the fungi.

Navigation

Foraging ants travel distances of up to 200 metres (700 ft) from their nest and scent trails allow them to find their way back even in the dark. In hot and arid regions, day-foraging ants face death by desiccation, so the ability to find the shortest route back to the nest reduces that risk. Diurnal desert ants of the genus *Cataglyphis* such as the Sahara desert ant navigate by keeping track of direction as well as distance travelled. Distances travelled are measured using an internal pedometer that keeps count of the steps taken and also by evaluating the movement of objects in their visual field (optical flow).

Directions are measured using the position of the sun. They integrate this information to find the shortest route back to their nest. Like all ants, they can also make use of visual landmarks when available as well as olfactory and tactile cues to navigate. Some species of ant are able to use the Earth's magnetic field for navigation. The compound eyes of ants have specialised cells that detect polarised light from the Sun, which is used to determine direction.

These polarization detectors are sensitive in the ultraviolet region of the light spectrum. In some army ant species, a group of foragers who become separated from the main column sometimes may turn back on themselves and form a circular ant mill.

The workers may then run around continuously until they die of exhaustion. Such wheels have been observed in other ant species, notably when a group has fallen into or been overcome with water, whereby the group rotates in a partially submerged circle on the surface of the water. The behavior could allow survival of a brief flooding.

Locomotion

The female worker ants do not have wings and reproductive females lose their wings after their mating flights in order to begin their colonies. Therefore, unlike their wasp ancestors, most ants travel by walking. Some species are capable of leaping. For example, Jerdon's jumping ant (*Harpegnathos saltator*) is able to jump by synchronising the action of its mid and hind pairs of legs. There are several species of gliding ant including *Cephalotes atratus*; this may be a common trait among most arboreal ants. Ants with this ability are able to control the direction of their descent while falling.

Other species of ants can form chains to bridge gaps over water, underground, or through spaces in vegetation. Some species also form floating rafts that help them survive floods. These rafts may also have a role in allowing ants to colonise islands. *Polyrhachis sokolova*, a species of ant found in Australian mangrove swamps, can swim and live in underwater nests. Since they lack gills, they go to trapped pockets of air in the submerged nests to breathe.

Cooperation and Competition

Not all ants have the same kind of societies. The Australian bulldog ants are among the biggest and most basal of ants. Like virtually all ants, they are eusocial, but their social behaviour is poorly developed compared to other species. Each individual hunts alone, using her large eyes instead of chemical senses to find prey.

Some species (such as *Tetramorium caespitum*) attack and take over neighbouring ant colonies. Others are less expansionist, but just as aggressive; they invade colonies to steal eggs or larvae, which they either eat or raise as workers or slaves. Extreme specialists among these slave-raiding ants, such as the Amazon ants, are incapable of feeding themselves and need captured workers to survive. Captured workers of the enslaved species *Temnothorax* have evolved a counter strategy, destroying just the female pupae of the slave-making *Protomognathus americanus*, but sparing the males (who don't take part in slave-raiding as adults).

Ants identify kin and nestmates through their scent, which comes from hydrocarbon-laced secretions that coat their exoskeletons. If an ant is separated from its original colony, it will eventually lose the colony scent. Any ant that enters a colony without a matching scent will be attacked. Also, the reason why two separate colonies of ants will attack each other even if they are of the same species is because the genes responsible for pheromone production are different between them. The argentine ant, however, does not have this characteristic, due to lack of genetic diversity, and has become a global pest because of it.

Parasitic ant species enter the colonies of host ants and establish themselves as social parasites; species such as *Strumigenys xenos* are entirely parasitic and do not have workers, but instead, rely on the food gathered by their *Strumigenys perplexa* hosts. This form of parasitism is seen across many ant genera, but the parasitic ant is usually a species that is closely related to its host. A variety of methods are employed to enter the nest of the host ant. A parasitic queen may enter the host nest before the first brood has hatched, establishing herself prior to development of a colony scent. Other species use pheromones to confuse the host ants or to trick them into carrying the parasitic queen into the nest. Some simply fight their way into the nest.

A conflict between the sexes of a species is seen in some species of ants with these reproductives apparently competing to produce offspring that are as closely related to them as possible. The most extreme form involves the production of clonal offspring. An extreme of sexual conflict is seen in *Wasmannia auropunctata*, where the queens produce diploid daughters by thelytokous parthenogenesis and males produce clones by a process whereby a diploid egg loses its maternal contribution to produce haploid males who are clones of the father.

Relationships with other Organisms

Ants form symbiotic associations with a range of species, including other ant species, other insects, plants, and fungi. They also are preyed on by many animals and even certain fungi. Some arthropod species spend part of their lives within ant nests, either preying on ants, their larvae, and eggs, consuming the food stores of the ants, or avoiding predators. These inquilines may bear a close resemblance to ants. The nature of this ant mimicry (myrmecomorphy) varies, with some cases involving Batesian mimicry, where the mimic reduces the risk of predation. Others show Wasmannian mimicry, a form of mimicry seen only in inquilines.

Aphids and other hemipteran insects secrete a sweet liquid called, honeydew, when they feed on plant sap. The sugars in honeydew are a high-energy food source, which many ant species collect. In some cases the aphids secrete the honeydew in response to ants tapping them with their antennae. The ants in turn keep predators away from the aphids and will move the them from one feeding location to another. When migrating to a new area, many colonies will take the aphids with them, to ensure a continued supply of honeydew. Ants also tend mealybugs to harvest their honeydew. Mealybugs may become a serious pest of pineapples if ants are present to protect mealybugs from their natural enemies.

Myrmecophilous (ant-loving) caterpillars of the butterfly family Lycaenidae (e.g., blues, coppers, or hairstreaks) are herded by the ants, led to feeding areas in the daytime, and brought inside the ants' nest at night. The caterpillars have a gland which secretes honeydew when the ants massage them. Some caterpillars produce vibrations and sounds that are

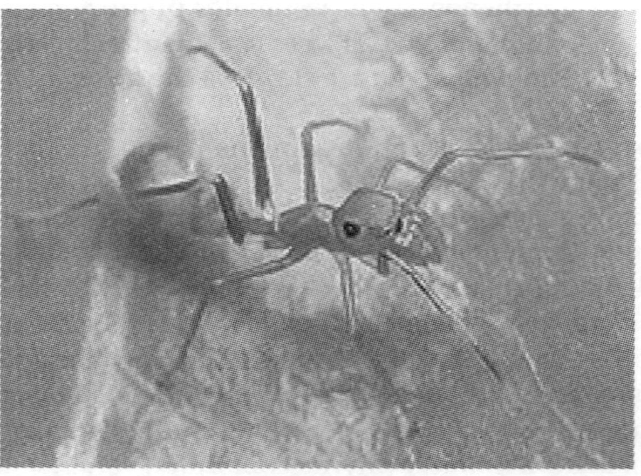

The spider *Myrmarachne plataleoides* (female shown) mimics weaver ants to avoid predators

perceived by the ants. Other caterpillars have evolved from ant-loving to ant-eating: these myrmecophagous caterpillars secrete a pheromone that makes the ants act as if the caterpillar is one of their own larvae. The caterpillar is then taken into the ant nest where it feeds on the ant larvae.

Fungus-growing ants that make up the tribe Attini, including leafcutter ants, cultivate certain species of fungus in the *Leucoagaricus* or *Leucocoprinus* genera of the Agaricaceae family. In this ant-fungus mutualism, both species depend on each other for survival. The ant, *Allomerus decemarticulatus*, has evolved a three-way association with the host plant, *Hirtella physophora* (Chrysobalanaceae), and a sticky fungus which is used to trap their insect prey.

Ants may obtain nectar from flowers such as the dandelion but are only rarely known to pollinate flowers

Lemon ants make devil's gardens by killing surrounding plants with their stings and leaving a pure patch of lemon ant trees (*Duroia hirsuta*). This modification of the forest provides the ants with more nesting sites inside the stems of the *Duroia* trees. Although some ants obtain nectar from flowers, pollination by ants is somewhat rare. Some plants have special nectar exuding structures, extrafloral nectaries that provide food for ants, which in turn protect the plant from more damaging herbivorous insects. Species such as the bullhorn acacia (*Acacia cornigera*) in Central America have hollow thorns that house colonies of stinging ants (*Pseudomyrmex ferruginea*) who defend the tree against insects, browsing mammals, and epiphytic vines. Isotopic labelling studies suggest that plants also obtain nitrogen from the ants. In return, the ants obtain food from protein- and lipid-rich Beltian bodies. Another example of this type of ectosymbiosis comes from the *Macaranga* tree, which has stems adapted to house colonies of *Crematogaster* ants.

Many tropical tree species have seeds that are dispersed by ants. Seed dispersal by ants or myrmecochory is widespread and new estimates suggest that nearly 9% of all plant species may have such ant associations. Some plants in fire-prone grassland systems are particularly dependent on ants for their survival and dispersal as the seeds are transported to safety below the ground. Many ant-dispersed seeds have special external structures, elaiosomes, that are sought after by ants as food.

A convergence, possibly a form of mimicry, is seen in the eggs of stick insects. They have an edible elaiosome-like structure and are taken into the ant nest where the young hatch.

Most ants are predatory and some prey on and obtain food from other social insects including other ants. Some species specialise in preying on termites (*Megaponera* and *Termitopone*) while a few Cerapachyinae prey on other ants. Some termites, including *Nasutitermes corniger*, form associations with certain ant species to keep away predatory ant species. The tropical wasp *Mischocyttarus drewseni* coats the pedicel of its nest with an ant-repellant chemical. It is suggested that many tropical wasps may build their nests in trees and cover them to protect themselves from ants. Stingless bees (*Trigona* and *Melipona*) use chemical defences against ants.

Flies in the Old World genus, *Bengalia* (Calliphoridae), prey on ants and are kleptoparasites, snatching prey or brood from the mandibles of adult ants. Wingless and legless females of the Malaysian phorid fly (*Vestigipoda myrmolarvoidea*) live in the nests of ants of the genus *Aenictus* and are cared for by the ants.

Fungi in the genera *Cordyceps* and *Ophiocordyceps* infect ants. Ants react to their infection by climbing up plants and sinking their mandibles into plant tissue. The fungus kills the ants, grows on their remains, and produces a fruiting body. It appears that the fungus alters the behaviour of the ant to help disperse its spores in a microhabitat that best suits the fungus. Strepsipteran parasites also manipulate their ant host to climb grass stems, to help the parasite find mates.

A nematode (*Myrmeconema neotropicum*) that infects canopy ants (*Cephalotes atratus*) causes the black coloured gasters of workers to turn red. The parasite also alters the behaviour of the ant, causing them to carry their gasters high. The conspicuous red gasters are mistaken by birds for ripe fruits such as *Hyeronima alchorneoides* and eaten. The droppings of the bird are collected by other ants and fed to their young leading to further spread of the nematode.

South American poison dart frogs in the genus *Dendrobates* feed mainly on ants, and the toxins in their skin may come from the ants.

Army ants forage in a wide roving column attacking any animals in that path that are unable to escape. In Central and South America, *Eciton burchellii* is the swarming ant most commonly attended by "ant-following" birds such as antbirds and woodcreepers. This behaviour was once considered mutualistic, but later studies found the birds to be parasitic. Although direct kleptoparasitism (birds stealing food from the ants' grasp) is rare, the birds eat many prey insects that the ants would otherwise eat and thus decrease their foraging success. Birds indulge in a peculiar behaviour called anting that, as yet, is not fully understood. Here birds rest on ant nests, or pick and drop ants onto their wings and feathers; this may be a means to remove ectoparasites from the birds.

Anteaters, aardvarks, pangolins, echidnas, and numbats have special adaptations for living on a diet of ants. These adaptations include long, sticky tongues to capture ants and strong claws to break into ant nests. Brown bears (*Ursus arctos*) have been found to feed on ants. About 12%, 16%, and 4% of their faecal volume in spring, summer, and autumn, respectively, is composed of ants.

2

Relationship with Humans

Ants perform many ecological roles that are beneficial to humans, including the suppression of pest populations and aeration of the soil. The use of weaver ants in citrus cultivation in southern China is considered one of the oldest known applications of biological control. On the other hand, ants may become nuisances when they invade buildings, or cause economic losses.

In some parts of the world (mainly Africa and South America), large ants, especially army ants, are used as surgical sutures. The wound is pressed together and ants are applied along it. The ant seizes the edges of the wound in its mandibles and locks in place. The body is then cut off and the head and mandibles remain in place to close the wound.

Weaver ants are used as a biological control for citrus cultivation

Some ants of the family Ponerinae have toxic venom and are of medical importance. The species include *Paraponera clavata* (*Tocandira*) and *Dinoponera* spp. (false *Tocandiras*) of South America and the *Myrmecia* ants of Australia.

In South Africa, ants are used to help harvest rooibos (*Aspalathus linearis*), which are small seeds used to make a herbal tea. The plant disperses its seeds widely, making manual collection difficult. Black ants collect and store these and other seeds in their nest, where humans can gather them *en masse*. Up to half a pound (200 g) of seeds may be collected from one ant-heap.

Although most ants survive attempts by humans to eradicate them, a few are highly endangered. Mainly, these are island species that have evolved specialized traits. They include the critically endangered Sri Lankan relict ant (*Aneuretus simoni*) and *Adetomyrma venatrix* of Madagascar.

It has been estimated by E.O. Wilson that the total number of individual ants alive in the world at any one time is between one and ten quadrillion (short scale). According to this estimate, the total biomass of all the ants in the world is approximately equal to the total biomass of the entire human race.

AS FOOD

Ants and their larvae are eaten in different parts of the world. The eggs of two species of ants are used in Mexican *escamoles*. They are considered a form of insect caviar and can sell for as much as USD 40 per pound (USD 90/kg) because they are seasonal and hard to find. In the Colombian department of Santander, *hormigas culonas* (roughly interpreted as "large-bottomed ants") *Atta laevigata* are toasted alive and eaten.

In areas of India, and throughout Myanmar and Thailand, a paste of the green weaver ant (*Oecophylla smaragdina*) is served as a condiment with curry. Weaver ant eggs and larvae, as well as the ants, may be used in a Thai salad, *yam*, in a dish called *yam khai mot daeng* or red ant egg salad, a dish that comes from the Issan or north-eastern region of Thailand. Saville-Kent, in

Ant larvae for sale

the *Naturalist in Australia* wrote "Beauty, in the case of the green ant, is more than skin-deep. Their attractive, almost sweetmeat-like translucency possibly invited the first essays at their consumption by the human species". Mashed up in water, after the manner of lemon squash, "these ants form a pleasant acid drink which is held in high favor by the natives of North Queensland, and is even appreciated by many European palates".

In his *First Summer in the Sierra*, John Muir notes that the Digger Indians of California ate the tickly, acid gasters of the large jet-black carpenter ants. The Mexican Indians eat the replete workers, or living honey-pots, of the honey ant (*Myrmecocystus*).

AS PESTS

The tiny pharaoh ant is a major pest in hospitals and office blocks; it can make nests between sheets of paper

Some ant species are considered pests, and because of the adaptive nature of ant colonies, eliminating the entire colony is nearly impossible. Therefore pest management is a matter of controlling local populations, instead of eliminating an entire colony, and most attempts at control are temporary solutions.

Ants classified as pests include the pavement ant, yellow crazy ant, sugar ants, the Pharaoh ant, carpenter ants, Argentine ant, odorous house ants, red imported fire ant, and European fire ant. Populations are controlled using insecticide baits, either in granule or liquid formulations. Bait is gathered by the ants as food and brought back to the nest where the poison is inadvertently spread to other colony members through trophallaxis. Boric acid and borax are often used as insecticides that are relatively safe for humans. Bait may be broadcast over a large area to control species such as the red fire ants that occupy large areas. Nests of red fire ants may be destroyed by following the ant trails back to the nest and then pouring boiling water into the nest to kill the queen. This works in approximately 60% of the mounds and requires about 14 litres (3 imp gal; 4 US gal) per mound.

IN SCIENCE AND TECHNOLOGY

Observed by humans since the dawn of history, the behavior of ants has been documented and the subject of early writings and fables passed from one century to another. Those using scientific methods, myrmecologists, study ants in the laboratory and in their natural conditions. Their complex and variable social structures have made ants ideal model organisms. Ultraviolet vision was first discovered in ants by Sir John Lubbock in 1881. Studies on ants have tested hypotheses in ecology and sociobiology, and have been particularly important in examining the predictions of theories of kin selection and evolutionarily stable strategies. Ant colonies may be studied by rearing or temporarily maintaining them in *formicaria*, specially constructed glass framed enclosures. Individuals may be tracked for study by marking them with dots of colours.

The successful techniques used by ant colonies have been studied in computer science and robotics to produce distributed and fault-tolerant systems for solving problems, for example Ant colony optimization and Ant robotics. This area of biomimetics has led to studies of ant locomotion, search engines that make use of "foraging trails", fault-tolerant storage, and networking algorithms.

IN CULTURE

Anthropomorphised ants have often been used in fables and children's stories to represent industriousness and cooperative effort. They also are mentioned in religious texts. In the *Book of Proverbs* in the *Bible,* ants are held up as a good example for humans for their hard work and cooperation. Aesop did the same in his fable The Ant and the Grasshopper. In parts of Africa, ants are considered to be the messengers of the deities. Some Native American mythology, such as the Hopi mythology, considers ants as the very first animals. Ant bites are often said to have curative properties. The sting of some species of *Pseudomyrmex* is claimed to give fever relief. Ant bites are used in the initiation ceremonies of some Amazon Indian cultures as a test of endurance.

Ant society has always fascinated humans and has been written about both humorously and seriously. Mark Twain wrote about ants in his book entitled *A Tramp Abroad*. Some modern authors have used the example of the ants to comment on the relationship between society and the individual. Examples are Robert Frost in his poem "Departmental" and T. H. White in his fantasy novel *The Once and Future King*. The plot in French entomologist and writer Bernard Werber's *Les Fourmis* science-fiction trilogy is divided between the worlds of ants and humans; ants and their behaviour is described using contemporary scientific knowledge. In more recent times, animated cartoons and 3-D animated movies featuring ants have been produced including *Antz, A Bug's Life, The Ant Bully, The Ant and the Aardvark, Atom Ant,* and there is a comic book superhero called Ant-Man. Renowned myrmecologist E. O. Wilson wrote a short story, *"Trailhead"* in 2010 for The New Yorker magazine, which describes the life and death of an ant-queen and the rise and fall of her colony, from an ants' point of view.

From the late 1950s through the late 1970s, ant farms were popular educational children's toys in the United States. Later versions use transparent gel instead of soil, allowing greater visibility. In the early 1990s, the video game SimAnt, which simulated an ant colony, won the 1992 Codie award for "Best Simulation Program".

Ants also are quite popular inspiration for many science-fiction insectoids, such as the Formics of *Ender's Game*, the Bugs of *Starship Troopers*, the giant ants in the film *Them!*, and ants mutated into super intelligence in *Phase IV*. In strategy games, ant-based species often benefit from increased production rates due to their single-minded focus, such as the Klackons in the *Master of Orion* series of games or the ChCht in *Deadlock II*. These characters are often credited with a hive mind, a common misconception about ant colonies.

3

Ants: Identification, Life-cycle, Habitat and Management

Ants are among the most prevalent pests in households. They are also found in restaurants, hospitals, offices, warehouses, and other buildings where they can find food and water. On outdoor (and sometimes indoor) plants, ants protect and care for honeydew-producing insects such as aphids, soft scales, whiteflies, and mealybugs, increasing damage from these pests. Ants also perform many useful functions in the environment, such as feeding on other pests (e.g., fleas, caterpillars, termites), dead insects, and decomposing tissue from dead animals.

There are over 12,000 species of ants throughout the world. In California, there are about 200 species but fewer than a dozen are important pests. The most common ant occurring in and around the house and garden in California is the Argentine ant, *Linepithema humile* (formerly *Iridomyrmex humilis)*. Other common ant pests include the pharaoh ant *(Monomorium pharaonis)*, the odorous house ant *(Tapinoma sessile)*, the thief ant *(Solenopsis molesta)*, and the southern fire ant *(Solenopsis xyloni)*. The velvety tree ant (*Liometopum occidentale*), nests in old wood and is a common outdoor species in landscapes.

Less common, but of great importance, is the red imported fire ant, *Solenopsis invicta,* which has recently gained a foothold in southern California. In some areas, the spread of the fire ant has been slowed by competition from the Argentine ant.

Carpenter ants (*Camponotus* spp.), also invade buildings in California. Although they do not eat wood as termites do, they hollow it out to nest and may cause considerable damage. For more information on carpenter ants.

IDENTIFICATION

Ants belong to the insect order Hymenoptera and are close relatives of bees and wasps. They are familiar insects that are easily recognized, especially in their common wingless adult forms, known as workers. However, winged forms of ants, which leave the nest in large numbers in warm weather to mate and establish new colonies, are often mistaken for winged termites, which also leave their nests to mate. Ants and termites can be distinguished by three main characteristics:

- The ant's body is constricted, giving it the appearance of having a thin waist; the termite's body is not constricted.
- The ant's hind wings are smaller than its front wings; the termite's front and hind wings are about the same size. (Shortly after their flights, both ants and termites lose their wings, so wings may not always be present.)
- Winged female and worker ants have elbowed antennae; the termite's antennae are not elbowed.

Ants undergo complete metamorphosis, passing through egg, larval, pupal, and adult stages. Larvae are immobile and wormlike and do not resemble adults. Ants, like many other hymenopterans, are social insects with duties divided among different types, or castes, of adult individuals. Queens conduct the reproductive functions of a colony and are larger than other ants; they lay eggs and sometimes participate in the feeding and grooming of larvae. Female workers, who are sterile, gather food, feed and care for the larvae, build tunnels, and defend the

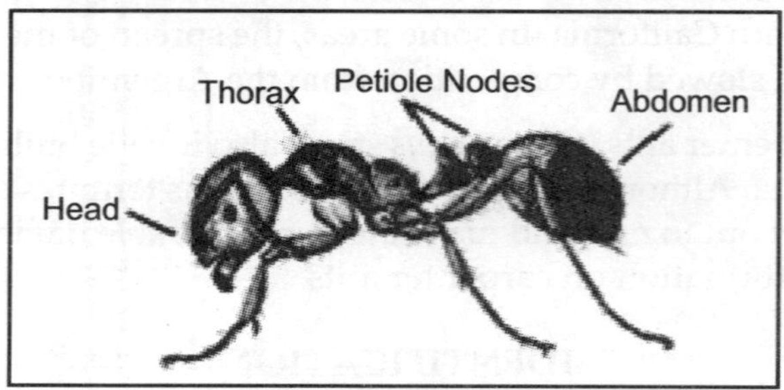

colony; these workers make up the bulk of the colony. Males do not participate in colony activities; their sole purpose is to mate with the queens. Few in number, males are fed and cared for by workers.

DAMAGE

Inside buildings, household ants feed on sugars, syrups, honey, fruit juice, fats, and meat. Long trails of thousands of ants may lead from nests to food sources, causing considerable concern among building occupants. Outdoors they are attracted to honeydew, produced by soft scales, mealybugs, and aphids. This liquid excrement contains sugars, and other nutrients. Frequently outbreaks of scales and aphids occur when ants tend them for honeydew because the ants protect scales and aphids from their natural enemies.

Ants can bite with their pincerlike jaws, although most species rarely do. The velvety tree ant, however, is an aggressive biter. A few ants sting, including native fire ants and harvester ants, which are primarily outdoor species, and are the most common stinging ants in California. An aggressive stinging ant, the red imported fire ant *(S. invicta)*, has recently been found in various southern California counties. If you suspect a fire ant infestation, report it to your county agricultural commissioner. For more information on red imported fire ants.

Life Cycle and Habits

Ants usually nest in soil; nest sites vary with species but are often found next to buildings, along sidewalks, or in close proximity to food sources such as trees or plants that harbor honeydew-producing insects. They also construct nests under boards, stones, tree stumps or plants, and sometimes under buildings or other protected places. In temperate climates the pharaoh ant nests indoors preferring warm, moist locations, often in wall voids, under flooring, or near hot water pipes or heating systems but is also found nesting outdoors in warmer parts of California. Ant food includes fruits, seeds, nuts, fatty substances, dead or live insects, dead animals, and sweets. Food preferences vary among ant species.

Ants often enter buildings seeking food and water, warmth and shelter, or a refuge from dry, hot weather or flooded conditions. They may appear suddenly in buildings if other food sources become unavailable or weather conditions change.

A new colony is typically established by a single newly mated queen. After weeks or months of confinement underground, she lays her first eggs. After the eggs hatch, she feeds the white, legless larvae with her own metabolized wing muscles and fat bodies until they pupate. Several weeks later, the pupae transform into sterile female adult workers, and the first workers dig their way out of the nest to collect food for themselves, for the queen (who continues to lay eggs), and for subsequent broods of larvae. As numbers increase, new chambers and galleries are added to the nest. After a few years, the colony begins to produce winged male and female ants, which leave the nest to mate and form new colonies.

Argentine ants differ from most other ant species in California in that their nests are often shallow, extending just below the soil surface. However, under dry conditions they will nest deeper in the soil. In addition, Argentine ant colonies are not separate but linked to form one large supercolony with multiple queens. When newly mated queens disperse to found new colonies, they are accompanied by workers rather than going out on their own as most other species do.

MANAGEMENT

Ant management requires diligent efforts and the combined use of mechanical, cultural, sanitation, and often chemical methods of control. It is unrealistic and impractical to attempt to totally eliminate ants from an outdoor area. Focus your management efforts on excluding ants from buildings or valuable plants and eliminating their food and water sources. Reducing outdoor sources of ants near buildings may reduce the likelihood of ants coming indoors. Remember that ants play a beneficial role in the garden in some cases. Become aware of the seasonal cycle of ants in your area and be prepared for annual invasions by caulking and baiting before the influx. Different species of ants respond to management practices differently.

Monitoring and Inspection

Monitor for ants near attractive food sources or areas of moisture. Ants may invade kitchens, bathrooms, offices, or bedrooms. Inspect under sinks, in cupboards, along pipes, and along electrical wires. Look for large trails of ants or for just a few stragglers. Straggling ants are scouts randomly searching for food or nesting sites. When you spot ant trails, try to follow the ants to where they are entering the building and to the nest if possible. Look for holes or cracks in foundations or walls that provide entry points to buildings.

Exclusion and Sanitation

To keep ants out of buildings, caulk cracks and crevices around foundations that provide entry from outside. Some caulking products available to professionals contain silica aerogel for long-term control combined with pyrethrins for more immediate effects. Ants prefer to make trails along structural elements, such as wires and pipes, and frequently use them to enter and travel within a structure to their destination. Indoors, eliminate cracks and crevices wherever possible, especially in kitchens and other food preparation and storage areas.

Store attractive food items such as sugar, syrup, honey, and pet food in closed containers that have been washed to remove residues from outer surfaces. Rinse out empty soft drink containers or remove them from the building. Thoroughly clean up grease and spills. Remove garbage from buildings daily and change liners frequently. Look for indoor nesting sites, such as potted plants. If ants are found in potted plants, remove the containers from the building, then place the pots for 20 minutes or more in a solution of insecticidal soap and water at a rate of one to two tablespoons of insecticidal soap per quart of water. Submerge so the surface of the soil is just covered by the water-soap solution.

Outdoor ant nests may be associated with plants that support large populations of honeydew-producing insects such as aphids, soft scales, mealybugs or whiteflies. Avoid planting such trees and shrubs next to buildings, or manage honeydew producing insects. Keep plants, grass, and mulch several inches away from the foundation of buildings because they provide nesting sites for ants.

Management on Trees and Shrubs

When numerous ants are found on plants, they are probably attracted to the sweet honeydew deposited on the plants by honeydew-producing insects such as aphids or soft scales. Ants may also be attracted up into trees or shrubs by ripening or rotten sweet fruit or floral nectar. These ants can be kept out by banding tree trunks with sticky substances such as Tanglefoot. Trim branches to keep them from touching structures or plants so that ants are forced to climb up the trunk to reach the foliage.

Protect young or sensitive trees from possible injury by wrapping the trunk with a collar of heavy paper, duct tape, or fabric tree wrap and coating this with the sticky material. Check the sticky material every 1 or 2 weeks and stir it with a stick to prevent the material from getting clogged with debris and dead ants, which will allow ants to cross. Ant stakes with bait can also be used around trees. In landscapes, some mulches can repel ants and discourage nesting. For example, aromatic pencil cedar mulch repels Argentine ants, whereas pine straw provides an ideal nesting site. Be aware that not all types of cedar chips repel ants: the effectiveness of red cedar chips found in California has not been verified.

Baits

Baits are insecticides mixed with materials that attract worker ants looking for food. They are a key tool for managing ants and the only type of insecticide recommended in most situations. Ants are attracted to the bait and recruit other workers to it. Workers carry small portions of the bait back to the nest where it is transferred mouth-to-mouth to other workers, larvae, and queens and other reproductive forms to kill the entire colony. Bait products must be slow-acting so that the foraging ants have time to make their way back to the nest and feed other members of the colony before they are killed. When properly used, baits are more effective and safer than sprays.

Baits are available in several different forms. For residential users, the most readily available forms are solids or liquids that are prepackaged into ant stakes or small plastic bait station containers. These products are easy to use and are quite safe if kept away from children or pets. Some products dry up rapidly and must be frequently replaced to control a large population. A few boric acid products are liquids that are poured into containers or applied as drops on cards.

Reusable bait stations, which are primarily available to pest control professionals, are more useful than prepackaged baits for difficult ant problems. Reusable stations can be opened, checked and refilled as needed. This is particularly important for liquid baits, which may be rapidly consumed or dry out. Some of these stations have removable cups that can be filled with two or more types of baits to offer ants a choice. Bait stations protect baits from photodegradation and disturbance by children. Some types of bait stations can be permanently installed into the ground or attached to outside walls or pavement in areas around schools or other buildings where ants are a frequent problem. They may be hidden in mulch so they are not immediately visible to children or pets.

Gel formulations of pesticide baits are packaged in small tubes. They are applied in small cracks and crevices where ants are entering. Gel products are now available to home users as well as professionals.

Ant baits contain either carbohydrates (e.g., sugars), proteins, or oils, or some combination of these as attractants along with an active ingredient (toxicant). Different attractants are more effective against different species of ants and at different times of the year. In the case of Argentine ants, sweet baits are attractive year-round. Protein baits are attractive primarily in the spring because they are brought back to the colony to feed the developing brood. In the case of fire ants, they prefer baits containing oils. Offering a small quantity of each kind of bait and observing which one the ants prefer is a good way to determine what to use.

Look for the active ingredient listed on the label of bait products. Some examples of active ingredients include hydramethylnon, fipronil, arsenic trioxide, boric acid (borax), avermectin B (abamectin), and n-ethyl perfluorooctane-sulfonamide (sulfluramid). Table 3.1 lists some common ant bait products organized by active ingredient. Bait products are constantly being improved. Look out for new active ingredients and improvements to current products. Avoid products packaged as granules that contain the active ingredients cyfluthrin or permethrin. Although these products may be

Table 3.1: Common Ant Bait Products Available in 2004. Effectiveness varies.

Active Ingredient	Example product name	Formulation: application/bait
Avermectin B (Abamectin)	381B Advance Select Granular Ant Bait	Solid: scatter or use bait station/protein
Borate-based products	Drax Ant Kil Gel[1]	Gel: apply in cracks/sugar
	Advance liquid ant bait[1]	Liquid: bait station/sugar
	Terro Ant Killer II Liquid Ant Baits[2]	Liquid: bait containers/sugar
Fipronil	Combat ant killing gel*	Gel: apply in cracks/protein
	Combat Quick Kill*	Solid: bait discs/protein
	Maxforce FC Ant Killer Bait Gel	Gel: apply in cracks/sugar
	Maxforce FC Ant Bait Stations	Solid: bait discs/protein
Hydramethylnon	Combat Source Kill*	Solid: bait discs/protein
	Maxforce Ant Killer Bait Stations	Solid: bait discs/protein
	Maxforce granular insect bait	Solid: scatter or use bait station/protein
Sulfluramid(N-ethyl	Advance Dual Choice ant bait stations	Solid: bait discs/protein or sugar
Perfluorooctane-	FMC FluorGuard Ant Control Baits	Solid: bait discs/protein or sugar
sulfonamide)	Hotshot MaxAttrax ant bait*	Solid: bait discs/protein or sugar
	Raid Double Control Ant Baits*	Solid: bait discs/protein or sugar
	Zep ant bait stations*	

*Available for nonprofessionals in retail outlets. [1]Orthoboric acid [2]Sodium tetraborate decahydrate (borax).

mistaken for baits, they are actually contact insecticides that rapidly kill foragers and do not control the colony. Likewise, bait stations with propoxur are not very effective because the active ingredient is too fast-acting.

To improve bait effectiveness, be sure to remove any particles of food or other attractive material from cracks around sinks, pantries, and other ant-infested areas. For the most effective and economical control, use baits only when there is an ant problem. Treatments made in late winter and early spring when ant populations are just beginning to grow will be most effective. Ant preferences can change throughout the year; to increase your success rate, set out different formulations of various bait products in a single baiting station, giving ants a choice. Do not use any insecticide sprays while you are using baits. Check and refresh bait stations regularly. Baits can dry up or become rancid and unattractive over time.

Use baits primarily outdoors. Use indoors only if there is a serious infestation and you can't find the spot where they are entering the building, otherwise you could actually attract ants indoors. Outdoor baits draw ants out of buildings. Place bait stations where ants can easily find them, but avoid placing them in areas that are accessible to small children and pets. Place baits near nests, on ant trails beneath plants, or along edges where ants travel. Space them every 10 to 20 feet outside around the foundation and at nest openings if they can be found. Effectiveness of baits will vary with ant species, bait material, and availability of alternative food. To achieve wide distribution of the bait so the entire colony will be killed, the bait toxicant must be slow acting. Control with baits is not immediate and may take several weeks or more to be complete.

Indoor Treatments

If ants can be thoroughly washed away and excluded from an area, an insecticide is probably not necessary. Vacuuming up ant trails or sponging or mopping them with soapy water may be as effective as an insecticide spray in temporarily removing foraging ants in a building because it removes the ant's scent trail, especially if thorough cleaning is done at the entry points. Some soap products such as window cleaners can kill ants on contact but leave no residual toxicity. Certain plant-based oils are also applied for this purpose, but their odor can be offensive.

Outdoor Treatments

A common method used to prevent ants from coming indoors is to apply a perimeter treatment of residual sprays around the foundation. Commonly used insecticides include the pyrethroids bifenthrin and lambda-cyhalothrin. Both are available in retail products, but products available to professionals provide a longer residual control than home-use products. Spraying around the foundation will not provide long-term control because it kills only foraging ants without killing the colony. Perimeter treatments may appear to knock down the population, but ants will quickly build back up and invade again. To try to achieve long-term control, some pest control companies offer monthly perimeter spray programs. Perimeter treatments pose more risk of environmental upset than baits in bait stations and are less effective than a bait-based IPM programme.

4

Ants of India

Ants occupy a great variety of habitats, with about 12,000 known species worldwide. Their biomass exceeds that of all vertebrates combined. Their social organization is orchestrated by intricate chemical communication. As central players in many ecosystems their species composition gives an indication of ecosystem health and functioning; while some are purists reliant on undisturbed ecosystems, others are weeds or even invasive. Their abundance and varied ecological roles make them influential in agricultural ecosystems around the world. Amid growing concern about biodiversity loss, some ant species and communities are at risk of disappearing; some even appearing on the IUCN Red List,while some invasives contribute to the extinction of other creatures. Improved understanding of ants, how to identify them, where they live, what they do is therefore a vital task in sustainably developing our world.

Ants are everywhere, but only occasionally noticed. They run much of the terrestrial world as the premier soil turners, channelers of energy, dominatrices of the insect fauna - yet receive only passing mention in textbooks on ecology. They employ the most complex forms of chemical communication of any animals and their social organization provides an illuminating contrast to that of human beings, but not one biologist in a hundred can describe the life cycle of any species. The neglect of ants in science and natural history is a shortcoming that should be remedied, for they represent the culmination of insect evolution, in the same sense that human beings represent the summit of vertebrate evolution.

ANTS: THE SUPER-ORGANISM

We humans recklessly crush tiny, but elegant ants under our feet unaware of the fact that these creatures are an important and indispensable part of our ecosystem. These tiny creatures have been on earth much before the arrival of human race. Ants originated 145 million years ago and were witness to the extinction of dinosaurs.

Since their origin, ants have evolved to become the most dominant creatures in terrestrial ecosystem. They constitute 25% of the total animal weight in the tropics. Because of their great adaptability, these creatures have occupied every possible niche or habitat found on land. They have colonized forest canopies, dug underground tunnels, made nest in rotten logs, crevices, etc. and braved the freezing temperatures of high altitudes to be part of high altitude ecosystem.

Ants are now-a-days considered as super-organism and this status has been well illustrated and described in recently released book on ants called "Super organism" by Pulitzer Prize winner writers E.O. Wilson and Bert Holldobler. According to them "a Super organism is a colony of individuals self-organized by division of labor and united by a closed system of communication."

Ant colonies display traits similar in function to the cells and organs of a bigger organism like humans. The function of an ant colony can well be understood by comparing it to a human body. The cells in a human body parallels colony members; organs parallels castes; gonads parallels reproductive castes; somatic organs parallels worker castes; immune system parallels defensive castes; circulatory system parallels food distribution including trophallaxis, distribution of pheromones and chemical cues, sensory organs parallels combined sensory apparatus of colony members; nervous system parallels communication and interaction among colony members and skin and skeleton of a human body parallels nest of these great creatures.

Ant colony is composed of millions of individuals and these individuals exhibit a variety of behaviors e.g. cooperation with nest mates, defending the nest from robbers, organizing food raids and finding the best food, tending the immatures in the nest etc; all targeted at improving the survival chances of their colony unlike most of the human beings, who are self centered, selfish and are always working for the downfall of their fellow beings.

Ant colony is built up by queen ant. After nuptial flight, fertile female ant finds a suitable nesting site for laying eggs. The eggs hatch into tiny larvae. The first batch of larvae is tended by the queen itself. The larvae change into pupal stage and finally the first batch of workers emerge. These workers then take up the responsibility of feeding the young ones i.e. the larvae as well as the queen. The worker caste works on the principle of division of labor and differentiates into soldier caste, foragers, feeders etc. In this way ant colony is established.

While performing all these tasks thousands of workers need to communicate for smooth functioning of the colony. The ants do not communicate verbally, or visually or with the help of auditory signals. These creatures use the language of chemical cues to communicate with each other. Ants release specific chemicals along with tactile cues (tapping each other's antennae) to elicit a specific response from fellow workers. These chemicals are called pheromones. They use blend of chemicals for recruitment of nest mates for collecting food; or to alert entire colony when attacked by intruders. Moreover, a unique colony odour is present in each ant's nest. The source of odour is the queen ant. All ants from one colony would therefore have a very similar odour and in this way can recognize nest mates from non nest mates.

By using these chemical signals ants remove dead bodies of fellow mates and debris to maintain hygiene of the nest, on contrary some species keep fragmented body parts of their colleagues as remembrance in their nests. Recently, it has been reported that like all other advanced mammal societies these creatures also show dominance and subordination and territorial behavior. Probably the ants have acquired these traits of behavior much earlier as compared to other animals including human species. Thus, the chemical signals act as a specific coded language conserving visual and auditory energy which even our human species cannot boast off.

Many other interesting behaviors are exhibited by ants e.g. some like *Harpegnathos* show jumping behavior, some feign death when captured, some show aggressive postures etc. Another form of behavior which is elucidated by many ant species like *Formica* (native to Himalaya and other parts of the world) is known as slavery. These ants raid other ant colonies capture their brood and workers, tame and use them for their own household chores.

Many of the ants have been grouped/classified on the basis of peculiar tasks performed by them. The major groups are:

1. Harvester ants
2. Weaver ants
3. Leaf- cutter ants
4. Army ants

Harvester Ants

The harvester ants have been named so as they harvest seeds of different types of grasses. These can be easily spotted in a garden, park or lawn where they create, corridors or passage on land which look like passages created by repeated movements of humans on grass lawns. These ants move in tandem, like many of the ant species have variety of worker force based on size and collect grass seeds. These bring grass seeds to their nest and store them in well kept godowns. Interestingly, harvester ants remove the plumule of seeds so that the seeds may not germinate in their nests and can be stored as food for long time. After consumption the hard seed coats are thrown out of the nests and can be noticed in abundance around their nests. Thus they help to maintain our terrestrial ecosystem.

Weaver Ants

As the name suggests they weave nest with leaves. One of the prominent groups in this category is red ant known as *Oecophylla*. These can be spotted on mango, citrus and guava trees and are quiet ferocious in nature. They don't nest in soil; instead exhibit marvelous architecture and intelligence to build their nest with leaves. The workers capture their little ones called larvae quite delicately in their jaws and move them to and fro on the edges of young tender leaves, in response to this movement or tricky feeling, little ones release sticky material from their glands. Then the other workers fold these leaves and join them with the secreted glue.

To join two leaves which are quite apart from each other, ants' form a chain by holding waists and thus pull the leaves together. This so called glue is known as silk (different from the silk secreted by silk worm). In mango or citrus orchards their nests are a delight to watch and even show great degree of sophistication as compared to bird's nests. They are a unique example of unbinding co-operation and high degree of unselfishness.

This group is well spread in South-East Asia. By occupying fruit-yielding trees these ants have shown tremendous potential in recent years to be used as biological control agents. The trees harbored by these ants show more fruit yield and produce healthy fruits. The red ants protect the fruits from other pests, thus ensure that their host tree is equally benefitted. In Thailand, Malaysia, some parts of Indonesia and Australia farmers and scientists are using these ants for production of better fruit quality and increase fruit yield. With expertise the nests can be easily shifted from one tree to another and these ants show remarkable adaptability to weave nests on the introduced trees. Other interesting aspect regarding these ants is that these are used in Chinese drugs, in soup and in some parts of South – East Asia their dried powder is considered as aphrodisiac. Thus like other ants weaver ants also ensure the survival of human race.

Leaf-cutter Ants

The ultimate super organism with best and most complex communication system known in animals, air conditioned nest architecture. Human agriculture, which originated about 10,000 years ago, was a major cultural transition that catapulted our species from hunter/gatherer life style to a technological and increasing urban existence, accompanied by enormous expansion of population.

Humanity thereby turned itself into a geophysical force and began to alter the environment of the entire planetary surface. Approximately 50-60 million years before this momentous shift, leaf cutter ants have already made the evolutionary transition from a hunter/gatherer existence to agriculture (Holldobler &Wilson in Super-organism). The leaf cutter ants cultivate fungi in their nests and are restricted in their distribution to New World.

These ants bring fresh leaves and plant cuttings into their nests; these are further cut into smaller and smaller pieces and are treated with ants' fecal liquid. Then these are inserted into that part of nest where fungus is cultivated. Fungus keeps on proliferating on these leaves and ants begin to feed on fungus. The fungus structures are rich in carbohydrates and proteins. Interesting aspect of the story is that even the most advanced human species if is forced to live with fungus culture may not be able to bear the brunt of pathogens but these super organisms are least susceptible to such infections.

The resistance developed is unparalleled in any form of life.The leaf cutter ants are of immense importance in tropical and sub tropical ecosystem and are also major pests in cultivated fields of Central and South America and harvest about 85-470 kg (dry weight) total plant biomass per colony per year. Probably, not feasible even for human species to harvest and process such enormous amount of plant material as carried by leaf-cutter ants.

Army Ants

It is a treat to watch a moving column of these ants in tandem and rhythm without exchanging a single word, can make the most efficient army of the world envious. Rarely you find that out of thousand to million of ant workers moving in a column get distracted or loose rhythm or direction. As the story goes, some of the workers of group *Dorylus* of army ants are great predators, many a times their attacks capture small mammals as efficiently as a python. In tribal Africa, mothers working in fields have lost their new borns to the marching column of these ants. They show tremendous sense of chemical communication and in some cases workers are blind. Some of these also act as pests of potato crop. Thus, army ant represent highest peak of togetherness and precision in attack and give horrified image to human species as a dinosaur would have given in its prime time.

5

Amazon Ant

Scientific Classification

Kingdom	:	Animalia
Phylum	:	Arthropoda
Class	:	Insecta
Order	:	Hymenoptera
Family	:	*Formicidae*

Species

- *Polyergus breviceps* western North America (probably includes several distinct species)

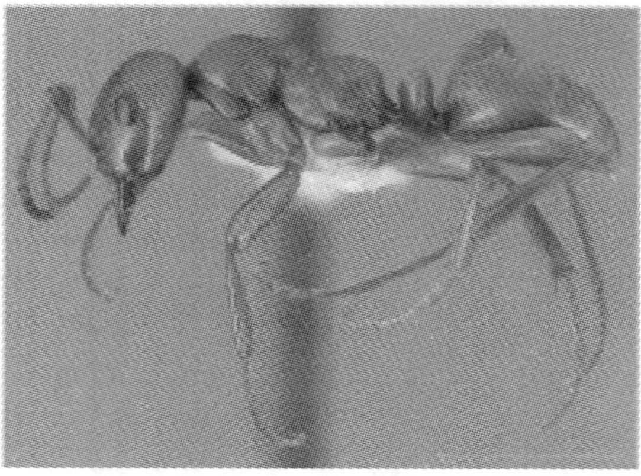

- *Polyergus lucidus* eastern North America to the Rockies
- *Polyergus lucidus longicornis eastern North America (considered a distinct species by knowledgeable myrmecologists, but this not yet formalized)*
- *Polyergus nigerrimus* Mongolia, Tuvan republic
- *Polyergus rufescens* Europe, western Asia
- *Polyergus samurai* Japan, Korea, eastern China
- *Polyergus texanus* (identity of this taxon uncertain, but unlikely to be a true *Polyergus*)

Name	:	*Polyergus rufescens*
Propagation	:	Europe
Queen	:	8-10 mm
Workers	:	6-8 mm
Food	:	Insects and honey water
Air moisture	:	50-70%
Temperature	:	20-30°C
Hibernation	:	Yes, from late October to late March at 5-8 °C
Nest-building	:	Soil nests
Formicariums	:	Tank, farm tank
Formicarium size	:	min. 30×20cm (adjust to colony size)
Particularities	:	Polyergus rufescens is also known as 'Amazon ant'. This species is a social parasite which keeps other ants as slaves. During spring and summer, these colonies carry out well organised raids on colonies of the Serviformica sub-genus. They steal their pupa and hatch them in their own nests. The hatchlings are unaware that they are

not in their original nest. They thus look after the Polyergus workers as though these were their own sisters, supply food and feed them. Polyergus ants are unable to survive without these 'slaves'. Polyergus are a beautiful red colour; their mandibles are sabre-shaped and therefore better suited for fighting. This species is only suited for experienced keepers and needs to be supplied with Serviformica pupae (Formica fusca for instance) on a regular basis.

Polyergus, also called Amazon ants, is a small genus of 6 described species (and several possible undescribed species) of "slave-raiding" ants. Its workers are incapable of caring for brood, in part due to their dagger-like, piercing mandibles, but more importantly, because in the evolution of their parasitism, they have lost the "behavioral wiring" to carry out even rudimentary brood care, or even to feed themselves. *Polyergus* species subsist solely as a specialized brood-acquiring caste, maintaining a worker force by robbing brood of particular species in the closely related genus *Formica* in massive colony-to-colony raids.

The captured ants are generally referred to as "slaves" in scientific and popular literature, though recent attempts have been made to apply other human cultural models, such as describing the *Polyergus* individuals of a colony as "raiders" or "pirates" and the *Formica* workers as "helper-ants", or "domesticated animals". Biologists describe the system simply as social parsitism by *Polyergus* on the host *Formica* species.

Polyergus obtains its *Formica* work force by stealing pupae from nearby *Formica* colonies and carrying them back to its own nest. Back in the *Polyergus* nest, *Formica* workers are eventually helped to emerge from the cocoons by *Formica* workers already living there. The new workers quickly assimilate the characteristic odor of the mixed-species population of the *Polyergus* colony—completely without violence. The *Formica* workers that emerge in the mixed-species colony go on to nurse, forage, and perform other colony upkeep duties.

As far as is known, all established *Polyergus* colonies have only one queen. To found a new colony, a lone *Polyergus* queen invades a nest of the host species, or encounters and moves in with a colony-founding queen of the host species and her first few workers. In the latter case, the host queen is allowed to survive until she has reared a number of host workers, something the *Polyergus* queen cannot do herself.

A young *Polyergus* queen kills the existing *Formica* queen (immediately if sufficient workers are present, later if these are not yet reared) and becomes accepted by the *Formica* workers. These proceed to rear the first and all subsequent *Polyergus* brood. Clearly, this complicated and lengthy process often fails, as *Polyergus* colonies are relatively rare, even though each mature colony produces dozens or hundreds of new potential queens each year. To counteract the natural mortality of the *Formica* worker population, *Polyergus* workers must conduct regular raids over a 6-8 week period, every summer over the 10-15 year life span of their colony

Habitat

Polyergus breviceps nest in a wide variety of habitats including meadows, other treeless habitats and open woods. Nests locations and its structure vary since these characteristics are dependant on the Formica species that Polyergus breviceps queens exploit. This host species can vary from habitat to habitat and between different portions of its range.

Etymology

Morphology: L. brevis short + L. -ceps head

IDENTIFICATION

Medium large workers with distinctive sickle shaped mandibles that have no teeth. Colour varies from concolorous yellowish-red to individuals with a deeper red head and thorax, and a dusky red gaster.

BIOLOGY

Polyergus breviceps are obligate slave makers. Workers raid nests of Formica species to steal their brood and pupae. Most of these stolen ants are used for food but some of the pupae are left to eclose in the Polyergus nest. These ants join other workers in carrying out of most of the tasks within the colony. This includes feeding the Polyergus adults, brood, and queen, tending the queen, managing all aspects of brood care and performing nest maintenance. The only roles not filled by the foreign workers are egg laying and raiding.

DISTRIBUTION

Range

Canada and United States. Ontario and Michigan westward to British Columbia and southwestward to Indiana, Illinois, Missouri, Kansas, New Mexico, Arizona, Nevada, and California.

Raids

Raids are carried out in the late afternoon, beginning with a growing group of frenetic workers gathering outside of and circling their own nest. Prior to this time a small number of scouts have been searching the local area for foreign nests to raid. A returning scouts emits pheromones that induce some workers to follow its lead, which is immediately followed up by all the workers circling the nest en masse and then moving off in a single direction. Additional workers will also follow up

this initial burst of workers away from the colony and join the raiding party. This mass of workers moves as a fairly cohesive group that can travel at a rate of 2 to 3 m per minute. The scout returns to the foreign nest using visual cues for guidance. As the scout leads the raid, the scout and other workers deposit a pheromone trail along the route being followed. From hundreds to more than two thousand individuals can take part in a raid.

Once reaching the nest of the foreign species workers search for and, once found, begin entering the nest entrance. Soon thereafter individuals exit the nest carrying a larva or pupae. Laden Polyergus workers begin running back to their own colony, following the same route they used for their arrival. Other workers need to wait for others entering, and then exiting, the colony before they can enter the foreign nest. Workers carrying stolen brood may be able to make it back to their own colony before all the raiding ants have made their way into the foreign nest.

Raids typically are completed within an hour and can secure from hundreds to thousands of stolen larvea and pupae. In cases where an attacked colony is particularly large the raid may be extended over a longer period of time. Individuals may make two round trips to the attacked nest. The number of raids carried out over the course of a year (from none to dozens) suggests the stimulus for raiding is the need for more workers. The majority of raids end without the raiding ants locating a colony of a foreign species. In unsuccessful raids workers stop advancing, milling about in a particular area where they are apparently searching for a non-existent or simply unfound nest entrance. After a few minutes of milling about an incohesive retreat back to the home colony begins. Through time more and more workers join in returning to the nest once the raid abandonment process begins.

Nest Founding

New queens may exit their natal nest with a raiding column, mate with a male while in the column and then attempt to enter the nest of a Formica species. If successful, she will eventually kill the host queen and any remaining Formica workers will stay with the colony and care for her Polyergus brood.

6
Argentine Ant

Scientific Classification

Kingdom	:	Animalia
Phylum	:	Arthropoda
Class	:	Insecta
Order	:	Hymenoptera
Family	:	Formicidae
Subfamily	:	Dolichoderinae
Tribe	:	Dolichoderini
Genus	:	*Linepithema*
Species	:	*L. humile*
Binomial name	:	*Linepithema humile* (Mayr, 1868)

The Argentine ant, *Linepithema humile* (formerly Iridomyrmex humilis), is a dark ant native to northern Argentina, Uruguay, Paraguay, and southern Brazil. It is an invasive species that has been established in many Mediterranean climate areas, inadvertently introduced by humans to many places, including South Africa, New Zealand, Japan, Easter Island, Australia, Hawaii, Europe, and the United States.

DESCRIPTION

Size	:	1/16" to 1/4"
Shape	:	Segmented, Oval
Colour	:	Dark brown to black and shiny
Legs	:	6
Wings	:	Varies
Antenna	:	Yes

The worker ants are about 3 millimetres (0.12 in) long and can easily squeeze through cracks and holes no more than 1 millimetre (0.039 in) in size. Queens are two to four times the length of workers. These ants will set up quarters in the ground, in cracks in concrete walls, in spaces between boards and timbers, even among belongings in human dwellings. In natural areas, they generally nest shallowly in loose leaf litter or beneath small stones, due to their poor ability to dig deeper nests. However, if a deeper nesting ant species abandons their nest, Argentine ant colonies will readily take over the space.

German entomologist Dr. Gustav L. Mayr identified the first specimens of *Hypoclinea humilis* in the vicinity of Buenos Aires, Argentina in 1866. This species was shortly transferred to the genus *Iridomyrmex*, and finally to *Linepithema* in the early 1990s.

Diet

Argentine Ants prefer sweet substances but will eat almost anything including meats, eggs, oils and fats. Also, when foraging for food, Argentine ants leave pheromone trails everywhere they go, instead of just from nest to food source. This habit ensures they do not waste time visiting the same area twice. While in other ant species worker ants are primarily responsible for gather food, Argentine queens also assist with foraging for food.

Habitat

Argentine ant colonies are located in wet environments near a food source. These colonies can grow to monumental size, sometimes covering entire habitats, such as an entire garden or your whole back yard.

Impact

Argentine ants do not pose a health threat, but they can contaminate food by leaving their bodily waste behind.

Global "mega-colony"

According to research published in *Insectes Sociaux* in 2009, it was discovered that ants from three Argentine ant supercolonies in America, Europe, and Japan, that were previously thought to be separate, were in fact most likely to be genetically related. The three colonies in question were one in Europe, stretching 6,000 km (3,700 mi) along the Mediterranean coast, the "Californian large" colony, stretching 900 km (560 mi) along the coast of California, and a third on the west coast of Japan.

Based on a similarity in the chemical profile of hydrocarbons on the cuticles of the ants from each colony, and on the ants' non-aggressive and grooming behaviour when interacting, compared to their behaviour when mixing with ants from other super-colonies from the coast of Catalonia in Spain and from Kobe in Japan, researchers concluded that the three colonies studied actually represented a single global super-colony.

The researchers stated that "enormous extent of this population is paralleled only by human society", and had probably been spread and maintained by human travel.

Behaviour

They have been extraordinarily successful, in part, because different nests of the introduced Argentine ants seldom attack or compete with each other, unlike most other species of ant. In their introduced range, their genetic makeup is so uniform that individuals from one nest can mingle in a neighboring nest without being attacked. Thus, in most of their introduced range they form supercolonies. "Some ants have an extraordinary social organization, called unicoloniality, whereby individuals mix freely among physically separated nests. This type of social organization is not only a key attribute responsible for the ecological domination of these ants, but also an evolutionary paradox and a potential problem for kin selection theory because relatedness between nest mates is effectively zero." In contrast, native populations are more genetically diverse, genetically differentiated (among colonies and across space), and form colonies that are much smaller than the supercolonies that dominate the introduced range. Argentine ants in their native South America also co-exist with many other species of ants, and do not attain the high population densities that characterize introduced populations.

Reproduction

Like workers in many other ant species, Argentine ant workers are unable to lay reproductive eggs but can direct the development of eggs into reproductive females; the production of males appears to be controlled by the amount of food available to the larvae. The queens seldom or never disperse in winged form. Instead, colonies reproduce by budding off into new units. As few as ten workers and a single queen can establish a new colony.

Impact

The ants are ranked among the world's 100 worst animal invaders. In its introduced range, the Argentine ant often displaces most or all native ants. This can, in turn, imperil other species in the ecosystem, such as native plants that depend on native ants for seed dispersal, or lizards that depend on native ants for food. For example, the recent severe decline in coastal horned lizards in southern California is closely tied to Argentine ants displacing native ant species on which the lizards feed.

Argentine ants sometimes tend aphid colonies, and their protection of this plant pest can cause problems in agricultural areas by protecting plant pests from predators and parasitoids. In return for this protection the ants receive a food as an excretion, known as honeydew. Thus, when Argentine ants invade an agricultural area, the population densities of these plant parasites increase and so too does the damage they cause to crops.

Pest control

Argentine ants accessing a commercial bait station commonly available in the United States. Within two days of this photograph, the ant colony appeared to have been destroyed and had ceased to access the five bait stations which had been placed.

Argentine ants are a common household pest, often entering structures in search of food or water (particularly during dry or hot weather), or to escape flooded nests during periods of heavy rainfall. Argentine ant colonies almost invariably have many reproductive queens, as many as eight for every 1,000 workers, so eliminating a single queen does not stop the colony's ability to breed. When they invade a kitchen, it is not uncommon to see two or three queens foraging along with the workers.

Due to their nesting behavior and presence of numerous queens in each colony, it is generally impractical to spray Argentine ants with pesticides or to use boiling water as with mound building ants. Spraying with pesticides has occasionally stimulated increased egg-laying by the queens, compounding the problem. Pest control usually requires exploiting their omnivorous dietary habits, through use of slow-acting poison bait, which will be carried back to the nest by the workers, eventually killing all the individuals, including the queens. It may take four to five days to eradicate a colony in this manner.

Researchers from the University of California, Irvine, have developed a way to use the scent of Argentine ants against them. The exoskeletons of the ants are covered with a hydrocarbon-laced secretion. They made a compound that is different, but similar, to the one that coats the ants. If the chemical is applied to an ant, the other members of the colony will kill it. The chemical method may be effective in combination with other methods.

Foraging Characteristics

Medium sized ant with a slender body, uniformly light brown or brown. Workers smell stale, greasy, or musty when crushed. Workers often present in large numbers moving in trails. Trails may be similar to white-footed ant trails, but ants are more slender and move more quickly so foraging trails may not appear as condensed. Workers may overwhelm outdoor eating areas, even entering parked cars.

7

Army Ant

Common Name : Army Ants

Order Name : Hymenoptera

Family Name : Formicidae

The name army ant (*Eciton burchellii*) (or legionary ant or "Marabunta") is applied to over 200 ant species, in different lineages, due to their aggressive predatory foraging groups, known as "raids", in which huge numbers of ants forage simultaneously over a certain area, *en masse*.

Another shared feature is that, unlike most ant species, army ants do not construct permanent nests; an army ant colony moves almost incessantly over the time it exists. All species are members of the true ant family, Formicidae, but there are several groups that have independently evolved the same basic behavioral and ecological syndrome. This syndrome is often referred to as "legionary behavior", and is an example of convergent evolution.

Most New World army ants belong to the subfamily Ecitoninae which contains the two groups, the Cheliomyrmecini and Ecitonini. The former contains only the genus *Cheliomyrmex* whereas the latter Ecitonini contains four genera, *Neivamyrmex, Nomamyrmex, Labidus,* and *Eciton*. The largest genus is *Neivamyrmex* which contains more than 120 species. But the most predominant species is *Eciton burchellii* of the genus *Eciton*; its common name "army ant" is considered to be the archetype of the species. Old World army ants are divided between Aenictini and Dorylini. The Aenictini contains more than 50 species of army ant in the single genus, *Aenictus*. However the Dorylini contains the *Dorylus*, these are the most aggressive species of driver ants, there are 60 species known.

Originally the Old World and New World lineages of Army Ant were thought to have evolved independently, an example of convergent evolution. However in 2003, genetic analysis of various species suggest that they all evolved from a single common ancestor which lived approximately 100 million years ago at the time of the separation of the continents of Africa and America. Army ant taxonomy remains ever-changing, and genetic analysis will continue to provide more information about the relatedness of the various species.

Army ant is a name that people use for ants that move in a line killing every insect and small animal in their path. People use other names for these ants, including Driver Ants, Legionary Ants, and even Visiting Ants.

Scientists describe army ants as ants that have two characteristics: migration or nomadic lifestyle and group predation. There are actually several different species of ants that behave this way. Some live in Africa and some live in South and Central America.

Army ants live in temporary nests. They seldom make underground burrows like other ants. The temporary nests, or bivouacs, are places where the ants rest between their hunting raids. The bivouac might be inside a hollow log, or it might be out in the open.

The ants often make the bivouac hanging from a tree limb. Thousands of workers will link their legs and their mandibles (jaws) and make an enclosed hammock for the queen. Sometimes the workers enclose the immature ants inside the hammock as well.

The army ants stay in the bivouac for a few weeks. Once queen comes out of the resting place and the colony starts to migrate.

Some species of army ants migrate in line. Other species migrate in a fan-shaped wave of ants. Many thousand ants move at once. The soldier ants march at the side of the column to defend the queen.

During the march, some of the workers carry the immature ants. Other workers gather all the food that they can find. As they go, the workers kill every insect, spider, snake, and lizard in their path. Birds and animals hear the ants marching and try to get out of the way.

As they march, the ants can climb trees or shrubs. They have been known to go through houses during the march. The residents of the houses scramble to safety when the column of ants comes in. The people remove their poultry and livestock to a place of safety.

If there is a benefit for the people, it is that when they return home, there are no roaches or other insect pests in their houses! The ants eat everything that does not run or fly away.

Scientists are studying these ants to find out what causes them to migrate as they do. Scientists once thought that the army ants migrated when there was no food left in the area. Now some scientists think that the timing of the migration might be linked with the development of the eggs and the immature ants in the colony. They suspect that there is a connection between the queen's egg production and the colony's movements.

Habitat

While some ants form complex nests and galleries, other species are nomadic and do not build permanent structures. Various species may form subterranean nests or build them on trees. Nests can be found in the ground with craters or mounds around the entrance, under stones or logs, in logs, hollow stems, even acorns. The materials used for construction include soil and plant matter, and they are highly selective of the nest site; *Temnothorax albipennis* will avoid sites with dead ants as these may be indicators of pests or disease. They are also quick to abandon established nest sites at the first sign of these threats.

Some of the more advanced ants are the army ants and driver ants, from South America and Africa respectively. Unlike most species which have permanent nests, army and driver ants do not form permanent nests, but instead alternate between nomadic stages and stages where the workers form a temporary nest (bivouac) out of their own bodies. Colonies reproduce either through nuptial flights as described above, or by fission, where a group of workers simply dig a new hole and raise new queens. Colony members are distinguished by smell, and other intruders are usually attacked.

Weaver ants (*Oecophylla*) build nests in trees by attaching leaves together, first pulling them together with bridges of workers and then sewing them together by pressing silk-producing larvae against them in alternation.

Nomadic and stationary phase

Army ants have two phases of activity: a nomadic (wandering) phase and a stationary phase.

Nomadic phase

During the nomadic phase the ants move during the day, capturing insects, spiders, and small vertebrates. At dusk they form their nest, which they change almost daily. Some species protect their paths with soldiers. During their hunt they are accompanied by various birds, such as antbirds, thrushes, and wrens, which devour the insects that are flushed out by the ants. Among the army ants there are also species that only venture out at night. However, there have been no adequate studies of their activities. Of the army ants which are active during the day, the species *Eciton burchelli* and *Eciton hamatum* are the most studied.

Stationary Phase

The stationary phase, which lasts approximately two to three weeks, begins when the larvae pupate. From this point on, the prey that were previously fed to the larvae are now fed exclusively to the queen. The abdomen (gaster) of the queen swells significantly, and she lays her eggs. At the end of the stationary phase, the pupae emerge from their cocoons (eclosion). After this, the ants resume the nomadic phase.

Nesting

Army ants do not build a nest like most other ants. Instead, they build a living nest with their bodies, known as a bivouac. Bivouacs tend to be found in tree trunks or in burrows that are dug by the ants. The members of the bivouac hold onto each other's legs and so build a sort of ball, which may look unstructured to a layman's eyes but is actually a well-organized structure. The older female workers are located on the exterior;

in the interior are the younger female workers. At the smallest disturbance, soldiers gather on the top surface of the bivouac, ready to defend the nest with powerful pincers and (in the case of the Aenictinae and Ecitoninae) stingers. The interior of the nest is filled with numerous passages and contains many chambers with food, the queen, the larvae, and the eggs.

Food

The whole colony of army ants can consume up to 100,000 prey animals each day and thus can have a significant influence on the population, diversity, and behavior of their prey. The prey selection differs with the species. Underground species prey primarily on ground-dwelling arthropods and their larvae, earthworms, and occasionally also the young of vertebrates, turtle eggs, or oily seeds. A majority of the species, the "colony robbers," specialize in the offspring of other ants and wasps. Only a few species seem to have the very broad spectrum of prey seen in the raiding species. Even these species do not eat every kind of animal. Although small vertebrates that get caught in the raid will be killed, the jaws of the American *Eciton* are not suited to this type of prey, in contrast to the African *Dorylus*. These undesired prey are simply left behind and consumed by scavengers or by the flies that accompany the ant swarm. Only a few species hunt primarily on the surface of the earth; they seek their prey mainly in leaf litter and in low vegetation. There are about five species that hunt in higher trees where they can attack birds and their eggs, although they focus on hunting other social insects along with their eggs and larvae.

Raids

In their raids, army ants follow two patterns: column raids and swarm attacks. The species *Eciton hamatum* is a typical example of the column raider. In this type, the swarm members separate to the sides of the main route and make small foraging groups, similar to a tree with its branches. The individual side paths can be widely separated from one another. The tropical army ants such as *Eciton burchelli* opt for the swarm attack. They, too, have a main route in the beginning which is then separated out into many branches in a form like an umbel, but their side paths are close together and may cross each other many times, so that the individual teams effectively cover a large area. In this way the column can fan itself out to a width of up to 20 metres.

Usage and circumscription

Historically, "army ant" referred, in the broad sense, to various members of 5 different ant subfamilies: in two of these cases, the Ponerinae and Myrmicinae, it is only a few species and genera that exhibit legionary behavior; in the other three lineages, Ecitoninae, Dorylinae, and Leptanillinae, *all* of the constituent species are legionary. More recently, ant classifications now recognize an additional New World subfamily, Leptanilloidinae, which also consists of obligate legionary species, and thus is another group now included among the army ants.

A study of thirty species (by Sean Brady of Cornell University) indicates that the ecitonine and doryline army ants together formed a monophyletic group: all shared identical genetic markers that suggest a common ancestor. Brady concluded that these two groups are therefore a single lineage that evolved in the mid-Cretaceous period in Gondwana, and so the two subfamilies are now generally united into a single subfamily Ecitoninae, though this is still not universally recognized.

Accordingly, the army ants as presently recognized consist of the following genera:

Subfamily Ponerinae

- *Leptogenys* (some species)
- *Onychomyrmex*
- *Simopelta*

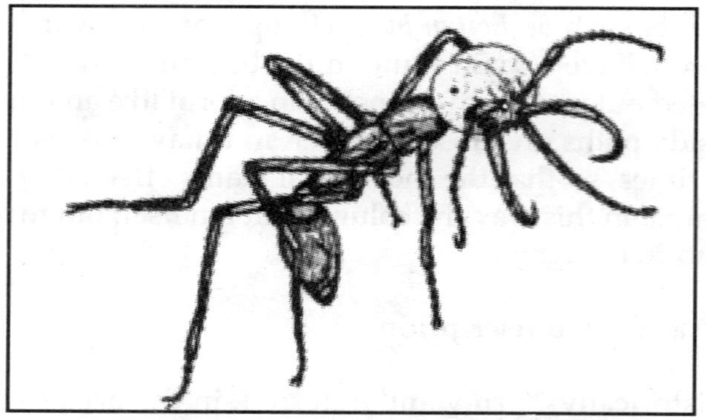

A soldier of the New World army ant *Eciton burchelli*

Subfamily Myrmicinae

- *Pheidolegeton*

Subfamily Leptanilloidinae

- *Asphinctanilloides*
- *Leptanilloides*

Subfamily Leptanillinae

- *Anomalomyrma*
- *Leptanilla*
- *Phaulomyrma*
- *Protanilla*
- *Yavnella*

Subfamily Ecitoninae

- *Aenictus*
- *Cheliomyrmex*
- *Dorylus*
- *Eciton*
- *Labidus*

- *Neivamyrmex*
- *Nomamyrmex*

Army Ants in Popular Culture

Army ants was a toy line in the late 80s. They were portrayed as cartoonish ants crossed with gruff characteristics of the US army; helmets, rifles and so on.

From:

The Amazon Basin. There's other subfamilies living in Asia and Africa, but these are the most notorious.

Why you must fear it:

By now, you will not be surprised to hear that these ants are, in fact, fucking huge, with the soldiers reaching a half inch in length. You will also not be surprised to learn that they have massive, powerful, machete-like jaws half the length of the soldiers themselves. They're notorious for dismantling any living thing in their path, regardless of size. They're also completely blind, which for some reason makes the whole thing worse.

They're called 'Army' ants because their entire colony, comprising up to and over one million insects, is a 100 percent mobile battalion. They don't make permanent hives like other ants, no, they bivouac down in single locations just long enough for the queen to shit out thousands of eggs, while the soldiers spread out in wide fans daily in search of food ("food" here, means "anything moving"). Then the eggs hatch and they enter the dreaded swarm phase of their existence.

8

Carpenter Ant

Scientific Classification

Kingdom	: Animalia
Phylum	: Arthropoda
Class	: Insecta
Order	: Hymenoptera
Family	: Formicidae
Subfamily	: Formicinae
Tribe	: Camponotini
Genus	: Camponotus Mayr, 1861
Type species	: *Formica ligniperda* Latreille, 1802
Diversity	: > 1,000 species

Description

Size	: 5/8"
Shape	: Oval
Colour	: Range in color from red to black
Legs	: 6

Wings : Varies

Antenna : Yes

Carpenter ants are large (.25 to 1 in/0.64 to 2.5 cm) ants indigenous to many parts of the world. They prefer dead, damp wood in which to build nests. They do not eat it, however, unlike termites. Sometimes carpenter ants will hollow out sections of trees. The most likely species to be infesting a house in the United States is the black carpenter ant (*Camponotus pennsylvanicus*). However, there are over a thousand other species in the genus *Camponotus*.

All ants in this genus, and also some related genera, possess an obligate bacterial endosymbiont called *Blochmannia*. This bacterium has a small genome, and retains genes to biosynthesize essential amino acids and other nutrients. This suggests the bacterium plays a role in ant nutrition. Many *Camponotus* species are also infected with *Wolbachia*, another endosymbiont that is widespread across insect groups.

Diet

Carpenter ants do not eat the wood they remove during their nest-building activities, but deposit it outside entrances to the colony in small piles. The diet of carpenter ants includes living and dead insects, meat, fats and sugary foods of all kinds, including honeydew and nectar from plants.

Habitat

Carpenter ant species reside both outdoors and indoors in moist, decaying or hollow wood. They cut "galleries" into the wood grain to provide passageways for movement from section to section of the nest. Certain parts of a house, such as around and under windows, roof eaves, decks and porches, are more likely to be infested by Carpenter Ants because these areas are most vulnerable to moisture.

As pests

Carpenter ants can damage wood used in the construction of buildings. They can leave behind a sawdust-like material called frass that provides clues to their nesting location. Carpenter ant galleries are smooth and very different from termite-damaged areas, which have mud packed into the hollowed-out areas.

Control involves application of insecticides in various forms including dusts and liquids. The dusts are injected directly into galleries and voids where the carpenter ants are living. The liquids are applied in areas where foraging ants are likely to pick the material up and spread the poison to the colony upon returning.

Exploding Ants

In at least nine Southeast Asian species of the *Cylindricus* complex, including *Camponotus saundersi*, workers feature greatly enlarged mandibular glands that run the entire length of the ant's body. They can release their contents suicidally by performing autothysis, thereby rupturing the ant's body and spraying toxic substance from the head, which gives these species the common name "exploding ants." The ant has an enormously enlarged mandibular gland, many times the size of a normal ant, which produces the glue. The glue bursts out and entangles and immobilizes all nearby victims.

The termite species *Globitermes sulphureus* has a similar defensive mechanism.

Selected Species

See below the list of *Camponotus* species :

- *Camponotus atriceps*: Florida carpenter ant; one of the many kinds of carpenter ants that can bite and release a painful acid.
- *Camponotus chromaiodes*: red carpenter ant
- *Camponotus compressus* (Fabricius, 1787)
- *Camponotus consobrinus*: sugar ant
- *Camponotus crassus* Mayr, 1862
- *Camponotus ferrugineus* (Fab.): red carpenter ant
- *Camponotus festinatus* (Buckley, 1866)
- *Camponotus flavomarginatus* Mayr, 1862
- *Camponotus floridanus*: a species whose genome was sequenced
- *Camponotus gigas* (Latreille, 1802): Giant forest ant
- *Camponotus herculeanus*
- *Camponotus kaura*
- *Camponotus ligniperda*: an important species in Europe
- *Camponotus nearcticus* (Emery): smaller carpenter ant
- *Camponotus novaeboracensis Region of Québec; black and red*
- *Camponotus pennsylvanicus* (DeGeer): black carpenter ant

- *Camponotus punctulatus* (Mayr): Tacuru ant
- *Camponotus saundersi*: Malaysia
- *Camponotus schmitzi* Stärke, 1933
- *Camponotus sericeus*
- *Camponotus silvestrii* Emery, 1906
- *Camponotus taino*
- *Camponotus universitatis* Forel, 1890
- *Camponotus vagus* Scopoli, 1763
- *Camponotus variegatus*: Hawaiian carpenter ant

Ants are divided into different castes, i.e. workers, queens, and males (Fig 8.1). Some ants, including carpenter ants, have polymorphic workers, which means that within one species the workers occur in different sizes. The best method to separate carpenter ants from other ants is by the following characteristics:

1) a waist with one node (petiole) and
2) a thorax with an evenly rounded upper surface (Fig. 8.2).

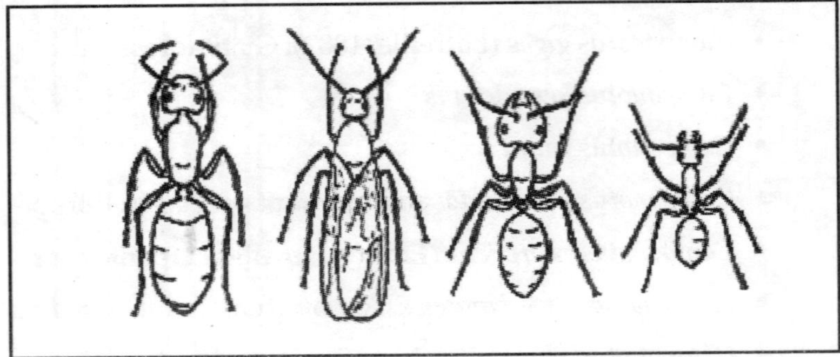

Fig. 8.1. Carpenter ant castes, from left to right: queen, winged male, major worker, minor worker

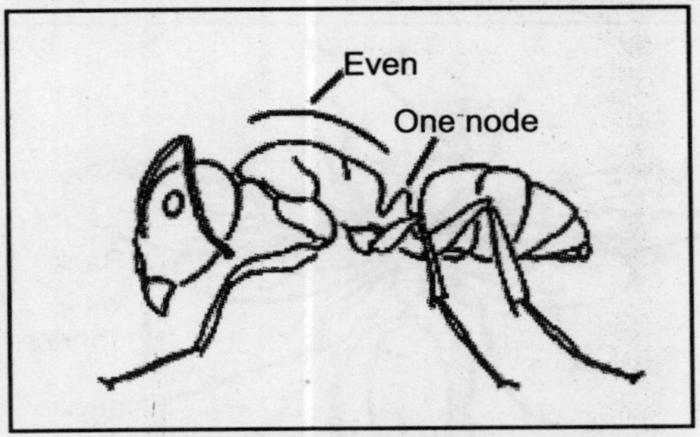

Fig. 8.2. Carpenter ant worker

There are other ants that appear similar and are occasionally mistaken for carpenter ants. They may have one or two nodes. However, they can be distinguished from carpenter ants by the uneven profile of their thorax (Fig. 8.3). These ants are usually not wood-infesting, so it is important to correctly identify the ants before control is attempted as control strategies vary with different ant species.

Ant or Termite?

Carpenter ants differ from termites by having dark-colored bodies, narrow waists, elbowed (bent) antennae, and if present, hind wings shorter than front wings (Fig. 8.4). Carpenter ants are very common and are frequently seen in the open.

Termites are light-colored, have no waist constriction, have straight antennae and, if present, wings are of equal length (Fig. 8. 5). Termites are much less common. They avoid light and are rarely seen outside of their colony.

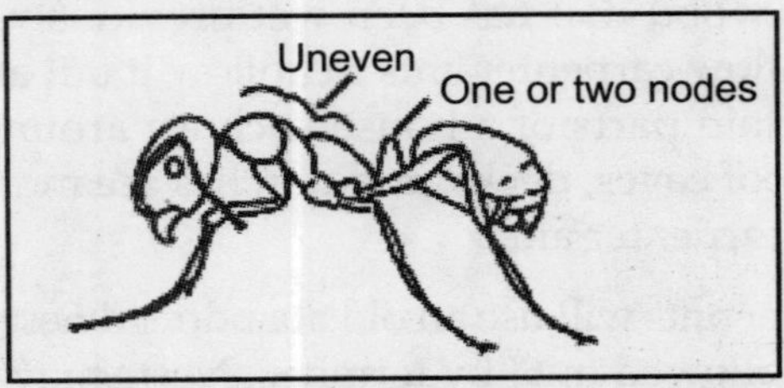

Fig. 8.3. Typical non-carpenter ant worker

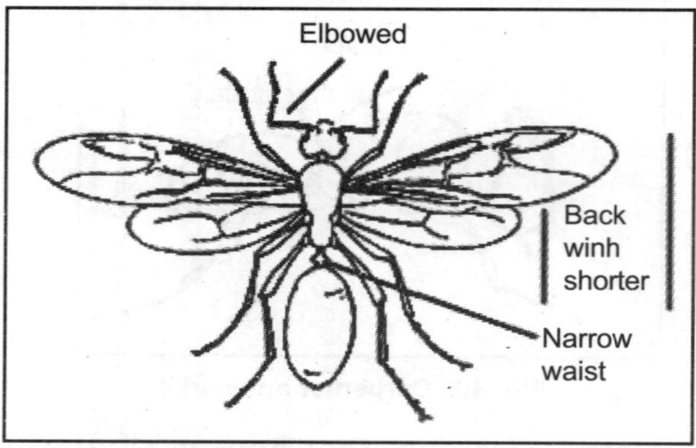

Fig. 8.4. Winged carpenter ant

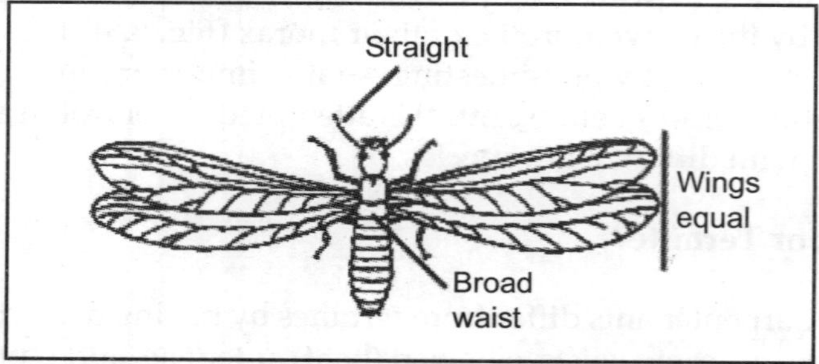

Fig. 8.5. Winged termite

Nesting

Carpenter ants construct their nests in hollow trees, logs, posts, landscaping timbers, and wood used in homes and other structures. These ants prefer to infest wood that is moist and rotting, but wood that has been wet previously, may be soft enough to allow carpenter ants to hollow it out and produce a colony. Certain parts of a house such as: around and under windows, roof eaves, decks, and porches are more likely to be infested by carpenter ants.

Carpenter ants will use an old abandoned nest or wood that has been "hollowed out" by termites. Nests may be located in hollow doors or small void areas produced during construction.

What They Eat

Carpenter ants feed on sources of protein and sugar. Outdoors, carpenter ants feed on living and dead insects. They are also very attracted to honeydew, a sweet liquid produced by aphids and scale insects. Aphids and scales feed on trees, shrubs, and other plants. Indoors, carpenter ants feed on meats, as well as syrup, honey, sugar, jelly, and other sweets. Carpenter ants DO NOT eat wood. They remove wood as they create galleries and tunnels.

Most foraging is done at night between sunset and midnight during spring and summer months. Sometimes workers travel up to 100 yards from a nest in search of food.

Where They Live

Carpenter ants nest in moist wood including rotting trees, tree roots, tree stumps, and logs or boards lying on or buried in the ground. They can also nest in moist or decayed wood inside buildings. Wood decay may be caused by exposure to leaks, condensation, or poor air circulation. Nests have been found behind bathroom tiles; around tubs, sinks, showers, and dishwashers; under roofing, in attic beams, and under subfloor insulation; and in hollow spaces such as doors, curtain rods, and wall voids. Carpenter ants may also nest in foam insulation.

A parent carpenter ant colony sometimes establishes one or more satellite nests in nearby indoor or outdoor sites. Satellite nests are composed of workers, pupae, and mature larvae. A satellite nest does not require moisture because the workers do not tend eggs (the eggs would dry out without sufficient humidity). For this reason, satellite nests can be found in relatively dry locations, such as insulation, hollow doors, and sound wood. The workers of satellite colonies move readily between their nest and the parent colony. In late summer, winged reproductives (i.e. queens and males) may emerge from pupae transported into satellite colonies. They may appear in structures in late winter and early spring as they swarm from a satellite nest.

Damage

Carpenter ants damage wood by excavating and creating galleries and tunnels. These areas are clean, i.e. they do not contain sawdust or other debris, and are smooth, with a well sanded appearance (figure 6).

The damage to wood structures is variable. The longer a colony is present in a structure, the greater the damage that can be done. If structural wood is weakened, carpenter ant damage can be severe.

Carpenter Ants During Spring

It is common to find carpenter ants in homes during spring. It is important to try to determine whether the ants are coming from an outdoor or an indoor nest, although this can be difficult. Their presence is not sufficient evidence to conclude that there is a nest in your home. You may be able to make a more accurate determination based on when you first see carpenter ants. If you find carpenter ants in your home during late winter or early spring, that suggests the ants are coming from a nest in the building. However, if you see activity later in the year, it is less clear if the nest is in the building.

Carpenter ants produce large numbers of queens and males during late summer. They emerge from nests the following spring for their nuptial flights. After mating, queens search for suitable sites to begin new nests. Once they land, their wings break off and each queen attempts to construct a new nest.

When carpenter ant nests are indoors, mating swarms become trapped inside. Finding large numbers of winged ants indoors is a sure sign that an indoor nest exists and may give the approximate location of the colony.

Finding one to several winged queens does not automatically mean a nest is present indoors. It is more likely the queens have just mated and have entered the home, searching for nesting sites. Wingless queens found walking indoors are new queens that have recently shed their wings but are still searching for nesting sites. They are not an indication of an indoor nest.

Carpenter Ants During Winter

In almost all cases, carpenter ants seen indoors during winter are an indication that there is an inside nest. One exception is when ants are brought indoors in firewood. Workers from firewood are not able to start nests in homes, nor do they damage wood structures in buildings.

Workers may become active during winter if the nest receives sufficient warmth from sunlight, mild outdoor temperatures, or from indoor heat. It is not clear whether just a few workers break dormancy or the entire nest becomes active. When ants are active during winter they will forage at night, searching for moisture. It is common for a home dweller to enter a room early in the morning, turn on the lights, and see ants scurrying for cover. Common places to sight them are cabinets, sinks, dishwashers, rolled-up towels, bathroom tubs, sink and toilet areas, or other places where moisture is abundant. On a bright sunny day, ants may be seen walking randomly through different areas of the house.

It is also possible for a carpenter ant nest to exist in a house during winter but not be noticed. If the nest exists at a site that does not receive sufficient indoor heat or sunshine, e.g. a north-facing outside wall, the ants will remain dormant until spring.

Prevention

An important method for preventing carpenter ant problems indoors is to eliminate high moisture conditions that are attractive to them. Also, replace any moisture-damaged wood. Be careful that wood or lumber that is stored in a garage or near the house is kept dry and, if possible, elevated to allow air circulation.

Store firewood as far away from buildings as possible. Remove tree and shrub stumps and roots. Trim branches that overhang the home.

Note: Be sure the tree or shrub species can be pruned at the time you wish; e.g., do not prune oak between April 15 and September 15 because of the risk of oak wilt. Also, prune branches that touch electrical lines or other wires that are connected to the house; carpenter ants can travel from branches to lines and use them like a highway to buildings.

Detection

In order to eliminate carpenter ants nesting indoors, you need to locate and destroy their nest.

The nest may be located by careful and patient observations of worker ants, especially between sunset and midnight during spring and summer months when carpenter ants are most active. To follow carpenter ants without startling them, use a flashlight with a red film over the lens—ants cannot see red light. You can increase your chances of following workers to their nest by setting out food that is attractive to carpenter ants. Place food in areas where you find workers.

- Many foods are attractive to carpenter ants, including honey or other sweet foods. During spring, carpenter ants are particularly attracted to protein sources, such as tuna packed in water. (Carpenter ants are not attracted to tuna packed in oil.) Set out small pieces of tuna for the ants to take back to their nest. It is easier to follow the ants when they are carrying food. With patience and perseverance, you can follow the ants back to their nest.
- Other signs that indicate an active nest is nearby include small piles of coarse sawdust or wood shavings, consistent indoor sightings of large numbers of worker ants, i.e. 20 or more, and large numbers of winged ants

indoors. Carpenter ants typically swarm from late winter through spring.

- Also pay attention to areas where steady moisture is or has been a problem; firewood stored in an attached garage, next to the foundation, along an outside wall, or in a basement; areas around the plumbing or vent entrances; and trees with branches overhanging the house. These are possible sources of carpenter ant nests.
- Sound detection may be helpful in locating a nest. An active colony may make a dry, rustling sound that becomes louder if the colony is disturbed. This sound, thought to be a form of communication, is made with the mandibles (jaws) and is not related to wood chewing. When trying to detect carpenter ants, tap the suspected area and then press an ear to the surface in order to hear any sound.
- If one nest is found, watch for evidence of additional nests. More than one nest may be present in a structure.

Control

The best method to control carpenter ants is to locate and destroy the nest, replace damaged or decayed wood, and, if they exist, eliminate moisture problems. Eliminating a carpenter ant nest is a difficult and challenging task. It is possible for a home dweller to control carpenter ants on their own. However, in most cases, control should be performed by an experienced pest control applicator. They have the experience and a wider array of products to more effectively control a carpenter ant problem. Home dwellers can still play a crucial role in control programs by providing information to a pest control provider, such as when, where, and how many ants were seen.

Indoors

Nests are often concealed in wall voids, ceilings, subfloors, attics, or hollow doors. It is usually necessary for a professional pest control applicator to drill small (about 1/8 inch) holes and apply an insecticidal dust into the nest area. It is best to determine the nest's location as specifically as possible. Control should not be applied randomly through the home. There are no insecticides available to the public that are labeled for this type of application.

If it is difficult to locate the nest, an insecticidal dust can be applied into wall voids through electrical outlets. Carpenter ants commonly travel along electrical wiring and are likely to encounter the insecticides. This method works more slowly than a direct treatment into the nest. Boric acid is available to home dwellers to treat wall voids through electrical outlets.

CAUTION: Use extreme care around electrical wiring and take all necessary steps to avoid accidental electric shocks.

If the nest is exposed (e.g. due to remodeling or reroofing) you can use a liquid or aerosol ready-to-use insecticide, such as bifenthrin, cyfluthrin, deltamethrin, or permethrin. Spray the insecticide directly into as much of the nest as possible. The more of the colony that is exposed, the better your chance of destroying it. It is necessary to anticipate a carpenter ant colony and have a product ready at the start of construction. Once the nest is exposed, that portion of the colony will try to relocate to protect themselves.

Sprays on surfaces where ants travel or congregate, such as along baseboards or in holes or cracks in the walls and floors, may reduce the frequency and number of ants you see. However, they are not effective in eliminating a nest because 1) the ants carry very little insecticide back to their nests and 2) most ants forage outside and do not come in contact with the insecticides.

Be aware of the potential for more than one nest in a building, but only treat nests that you know exist. Do not treat areas of a building if additional nests are not found. Once a carpenter ant nest is treated, continue to watch for evidence of an active nest until the following spring. If no evidence is observed, then further insecticide applications are unnecessary.

Baits

If the nest cannot be located, baits may be an effective alternative. Baits work by combining an attractive food source with a slow-acting toxicant. A delayed toxicant is critical because it allows the ants to forage normally for days or even weeks. During that time, ants consume the bait and return to the nest to share the bait with the rest of the colony. In a process known as trophallaxis, one ant regurgitates its stomach contents to another ant. This food sharing behavior enables the bait to be spread throughout the colony before the toxicant takes effect.

There are a few baits available to nonprofessionals for carpenter ant control. Most retail products are liquid or granular formulations containing hydramethylnon, sulfluramid, abamectin, or boric acid. Baits vary a great deal in their effectiveness. Carpenter ants have complex food preferences, and some of the sugar-based baits will not be attractive to the ants long enough to be successful.

The keys to successful baiting are placement and monitoring; a bait cannot be effective if it is never encountered by ants. Place the bait only in areas where activity has been seen or is strongly suspected. After offering the bait, monitor it over 24 hours for feeding activity. Any bait that is ignored should be substituted with another, and any that is consumed should be replenished. Remember that increased ant activity around baits is a good sign. Never apply insecticides on or around baits because this will prevent feeding and render baits useless. Do not spray or dust other areas of the home, especially where carpenter ants are seen, as this can reduce the effectiveness of the bait. Be patient—baits can take weeks or months to achieve control.

Professional pest control personnel are trained in baiting techniques and have access to a wider variety of products than consumers. They are more likely to achieve positive results. Contact a licensed pest control company if you prefer the expertise and experience of a professional.

Outdoors

Often carpenter ant nests found indoors are satellite nests that can be traced back to a parent colony outdoors in trees, stumps, roots, fence posts, landscape timbers, and other wood structures. When possible, remove wood that contains carpenter ant nests, or destroy the colony.

When this is not practical, and carpenter ants have been discovered entering your home from outdoor nests, a treatment with a residual insecticide around the building's exterior helps keep them out of your home. Products, such as bifenthrin, cyfluthrin, or permethrin, are available to home dwellers. Be sure the product you intend to use is labeled for use around building exteriors. Professional pest control services can also treat your home's exterior.

Spray the product in a band, covering the foundation and under the lower edge of the siding to help keep ants from coming inside. Trim branches that overhang buildings or electrical wiring to avoid giving carpenter ants easy access to your home.

Note: *Be sure the tree or shrub species can be pruned at the time you wish, e.g. do not prune oak between April 15 and September 15 because of the risk of oak wilt.*

Treating the building's exterior is a short term control measure. A permanent control method is to eliminate or remove the nest. If this cannot be done directly, then use baits to eradicate the outdoor colony.

In trees

Carpenter ants nest in trees in one of two situations: 1) in rotted, decayed wood or 2) in the center heartwood section of the tree. In neither case are they harmful to the tree. Control is unnecessary for the tree's health, as the ants are taking advantage of preexisting soft, weak wood to establish their colony. Insects, disease, or environmental conditions such as drought are often responsible for weakening and killing limbs or sections of trees. This allows wood rot to set in, which results in wood decay, giving carpenter ants the opportunity to colonize the tree. Carpenter ants use knots, cracks, holes, and old insect tunnels to gain access to these areas.

Control of carpenter ants in trees is warranted if there are indications that ants are entering homes from colonies in trees. If there is evidence of this, the best control is to bait the colony.

Colony Dynamics And Life Cycle

Carpenter ants feed on dead and living insects, nectar, fruit juices, and sugary honeydew excreted by plant-sucking insects.

They will enter buildings in search of nesting sites or moisture and can build nests containing several thousand ants. Typically, the nests they construct indoors are satellites of a larger, parent nest located outside in a live or dead tree, a woodpile, or landscaping materials. Several satellite nests can be associated with a single parent nest, where the queen or queens reside, as in the case of *C. vicinus,* which can have as many as 40 queens in a single nest.

New reproductives have wings and leave the nest on mating flights in the spring. The timing of these flights varies for each species. For example, *C. modoc* swarms in the late afternoon, often after a heavy rainfall. After the mating flight, males die, and inseminated queens disperse in search of potential nest sites such as a dead tree or stump. Here, the newly mated queen excavates a chamber, seals herself in, and begins laying eggs. Colony growth is slow at first and only after several years does the colony reach maturity and begin producing a new generation of winged ants to begin the cycle again.

MANAGEMENT

There are several nonchemical measures that can help prevent infestations:

- Trim tree branches and shrubs away from structures to prevent access;
- Seal off potential entry points such as where utility lines enter a structure;
- Reduce mulch around building perimeters to a depth of 2 to 3 inches to discourage nesting;
- Eliminate any earth-to-wood contact of structural elements that might promote wood decay;
- Replace decayed or damaged wood and correct problems that cause decay such as clogged rain gutters or leaky pipes;
- Increase ventilation to damp areas such as attic or subfloor spaces;
- Store firewood off the ground and several feet away from structures; and
- Remove potential food sources inside a structure and store them in tightly sealed containers.

Because ants have a "sweet tooth," reducing the number of insects that produce honeydew might control ants around structures. For more information on managing these pests, see *Pest Notes: Aphids, Giant Whitefly*, and *Scales*.

Impact

Carpenter ants don't carry disease, but when building a nest inside a home, Carpenter Ants dig smooth tunnels inside the wood. These tunnels weaken the wood and potentially damage the wood that keeps the house standing. This kind of damage can be very expensive to fix.

Prevention

- Eliminate standing water. Pests, such as ants, mosquitoes and termites, are attracted to moisture.
- Keep tree branches and other plants cut back from the house. Sometimes pests use these branches to get into your home.
- Make sure that there are no cracks or little openings around the bottom of your house. Sometimes pests use these to get into your home.
- Make sure that firewood and building materials are not stored next to your home. Pests like to build nests in stacks of wood.

9

Harvester Ant

Scientific Classification

Kingdom	: Animalia
Phylum	: Arthropoda
Class	: Insecta
Order	: Hymenoptera
Family	: Formicidae
Subfamily	: Myrmicinae
Tribe	: Myrmicini
Genus	: Pogonomyrmex
Species	: *Pogonomyrmex barbatus*
Binomial name	: *P. barbatus* Smith, 1858

DESCRIPTION

The main food source for red harvester ants usually consists of seeds, which they hoard in great numbers, hence their name.

As with most ant species, their mating castes consist of winged alates (reproductives) that reside in the nest until weather permits them to fly away and mate. After that the male

Red Harvester Ant

usually dies, while the now-fertilized queen returns to the ground to search for a suitable nesting site. Once she has chosen a site, she sheds her wings and begins to reproduce, creating a new colony. She produces "worker ants" for 1–20 years until her death.

Red harvester ants can be aggressive, and have a painful sting that spreads through the lymph nodes, sometimes causing reactions, especially in animals allergic to their venom. They can also bite ferociously.

Over the years, their numbers have been declining, and this has often been attributed to competition for food with the invasive red imported fire ant and the Argentine ant. Their decline has affected many native species, especially those for which the red harvester ant is a chief source of food, such as the Texas horned lizard. Red harvester ants are often mistaken for fire ants, but are not related to any fire ant species, native or introduced. This class of ants is also known to have both male and female genesis.

Red harvester ant nests are characterized by a lack of foliage and small pebbles surrounding a hole that is usually at grade. Hollowed out seeds, however, are found scattered around the nest. In grassland areas, such as ranches, the lack of plant life makes red harvester ant colonies very easy to spot. The mounds are typically flat and broad, 0 to 100 mm (0 to 3.9 in) high, and 300 to 1,200 mm (12 to 47 in) in diameter. There have been reports of even larger denuded areas, on the order of 10 m^2 (110 sq ft). Three to eight trails typically lead away from the mound, like "arms". These trails are used by ants to collect and bring food back to the mound. "Scout" ants are the first ones out of the mound every morning. They seek food, and mark their path as they return to the mound to alert the worker ants. The worker ants follow the scent trail and collect the food. Other ants, called "middens", spend their time cleaning and tending to the mound. All worker ants and middens are female.

The common species of harvester ants – the Red, Western, and California harvester ants each have unique behaviors, castes and tasks, feeding, nesting patterns and defense mechanisms. The harvester ant behavior differs between each species, seen through their feeding and nesting habits. In addition, unlike other ants that infest indoor structures, all species of harvest ants prefer not to invade houses and buildings, but will establish their nests around gardens or yards, often destroying vegetation. The red harvester ants can be aggressive. They give out a painful sting. Sometimes, the stings of red harvest ants can cause allergic reactions, especially to those sensitive to their venom. Aside from their powerful stings, the red harvester ant also bites viciously. However, due to the competition for food with the ferocious red fire ants, the population of red harvester ants appears to be declining. This is an important agricultural pest in many areas. The feeding habits of red harvester ants can be seen as they leave their nests and crawl to their food sources, leaving a distinct scent throughout their paths. Once the scent paths stop, the red harvester ants go their own ways and forage for food. The Western harvester ant is found in the west at high elevations. This is a red colored ant that can be almost one half an inch long. This ant can cause damage to highways by encouraging erosion under roads.

Galleries have been found to go over 9 feet deep. Leafcutter ants also have been considered harvester ants. They exhibit high degrees of polymorphism with castes including the minims, mediae, minors and majors. They are divided based on their size to perform different tasks. For instance, the majors are considered the leafcutter ant soldiers, while the mediae are known as the foragers of food. The minims tend their fungus gardens, while the minors guard the nest from predators. Leafcutter ants, particularly the majors, are strong enough to cut through leather.

Another group of harvester ants are the Messor harvester ants which have over 100 different species. Their colonies contain only one queen, but with hundreds of workers. The Messor harvester ants are known as sophisticated architects because of their intricately designed nests, wherein they store seeds during dry weather to avoid germs. Messor ants can easily cut through large seeds and carry them back to their nests. However, these harvester ants exhibit slow movement.

Pheidole harvester ants have three kinds of members within their colonies – the minor workers, soldiers or major workers and the queen. The major workers are known for their large heads that may give them a fierce appearance. However, these harvester ants are usually shy and often flee at signs of danger.

WESTERN HARVESTER ANT

Within the United States, the western harvester ant, or *Pogonomyrmex occidentalis,* is primarily seen in the mountain ranges of most of the western states. Unlike other ant species, the western harvester ant prefers to dwell in areas where the soil has already been disturbed.

Western harvester ants measure about 3/8-inch in length and are orange, red, dark brown or brown-black in color. Some may display multiple colors.

The nests of the western harvester ant measure one to four feet wide and two to 10 inches high. While they appear to be merely piles of dirt, the nests contain several interior chambers. Western harvester ants often remove all surrounding plants in order to prevent shade. These ants cover their mounds with charcoal, dead leaves, small rocks and other debris to keep them warm and they remain inside the nests during the hottest parts of the day. There have been reports of damage to pavement because of the mounds of Western harvester ants. The mounds were built at the edge of the pavement and caused erosion when it rained.

Western harvester ants feed on seeds and insects, but typically eat only one species at a time. Western harvester ants can travel long distances in search of food, and different species of western harvester ants exhibit different foraging behaviors. Red harvester ants leave scent trails of their routes, while California harvester ants leave their nests one at a time and go in all directions without leaving trails.

Some western harvester ant species are aggressive, fighting with members of their own as well as other ant colonies, while other western harvester ant species do not fight at all. Western harvester ants can be defensive of their nests when a threat is perceived.

This species swarms primarily during summer. Western harvester ants mate in flight and newly fertilized queens then begin their own colonies.

BLACK HARVESTER ANT

The black harvester ant is one of 22 species of harvester ants found in the United States. This ant is common from southern California to western Texas. Harvested seeds are the primary food source of the black harvester ant. These ants will collect a single seed or plant until the supply is exhausted, at which point they will begin harvesting another type of seed.

The black harvester ant's antennae consist of twelve segments without a club. Under the head is a row of long hairs, known as the *psammophore*. The thorax and head contain shallow parallel grooves, with a pair of spines located atop the thorax.

Unlike other ant species, black harvester ants do not nest inside other structures. Instead, they seek out areas, which are open and clear of vegetation. They build their mounds and cover them with gravel, charcoal, tiny rocks or fragments of dead vegetation. This debris serves as a solar energy trap, controlling nest temperature. Black harvester ant nests are excavated deep within the ground and may span 30 feet in diameter. Black harvester ants will relocate their nest once or twice each year due to climate changes.

Swarming black harvester ants are common during the summer. Soon after mating with ants from nearby colonies, male ants die and females land in search of new nesting sites. Colonies of black harvester ants are populous, but contain only one queen, who can survive up to 30 years.

Because they are desert dwellers, black harvester ants do not commonly encounter humans. However, they do sometimes build nests near human dwellings, and black harvester ants sting when disturbed or attacked by predators.

TEXAS RED HARVESTER ANT

In the United States alone, there are 22 species of harvester ants. Ten of these harvester ant species are found in Texas, and seven species are seen around the far western areas of Texas. Of all the harvester ant species in Texas, the Texas red harvester ant is the most noticeable: these large ants are typically seen in open areas. Texas red harvester ants are the most common ants sold to hobbyists who maintain ant farms.

Workers of the red harvester ant colonies have long bodies and range in color from red to dark brown. They have square heads and no spines on their bodies. Winged males and female swarmers are larger than worker ants.

Texas red harvester ants feed primarily on seeds, including wild sunflowers, Johnson grass, burr clovers, alfalfa seeds and other small beans. They also consume insects.

Red harvester ants mate after rainy days. Males die soon after mating, while females shed their wings and begin new colonies by digging a burrow and laying eggs within it. These eggs eventually become worker ants, which care for other developing ants, build the nest and forage for food.

The sting of the Texas red harvester ant is painful and can cause severe allergic reactions. Colonies of the Texas red harvester ant are also widely separated and can infest rangelands and pastures heavily, resulting in a decreased yield.

The Texas red harvester ant is the primary source of food of the Texas horned lizard. This lizard is a protected species. The spread of Red Imported Fire ants has resulted in a decrease in the number of harvester ant colonies. Although harvester ants can be controlled using pesticides, it is best to refrain from using chemical products, as these would also harm the Texas horned lizard population.

Life Cycle

Winged males and females swarm, pair and mate. Males soon die and females seek a suitable nesting site. After dropping her wings, the queen ant digs a burrow and produces a few eggs. Larvae hatch from eggs and developed through several stages (instars). Larvae are white and legless, shaped like a crookneck squash with a small distinct head. Pupation occurs within a cocoon. Worker ants produced by the queen ant begin caring for other developing ants, enlarge the nest and forage for food.

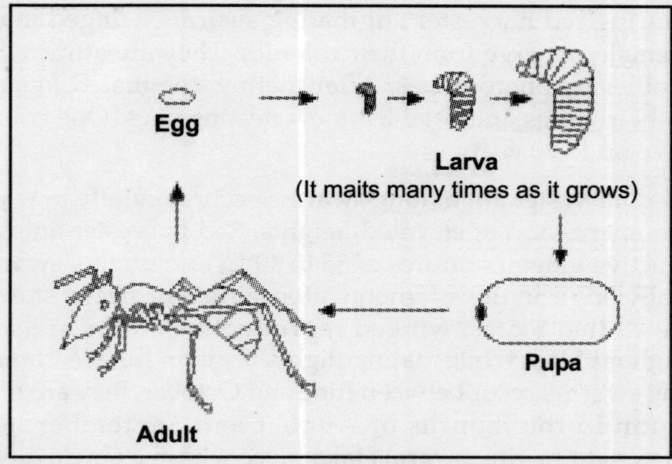

Life cycle harvester ants

Habitat

Worker ants remove vegetation in circular areas or craters around nests. Colonies occur in open areas and usually have a single central opening. The area around the opening usually has small pebbles deposited on the soil surface by the worker ants. Often there is no vegetation within a 3- to 6-foot circle around the central opening of the colony, and along foraging trails radiating from the colony. Colonies usually are widely separated; however, heavy infestations in pasture and rangeland can reduce yield. Red harvester ants also colonize in ornamental turf areas where their presence may be undesirable. They do not invade homes or structures.

Red Harvester Ant Mating Swarms

Like other ant species, red harvester ants are divided into castes within their colonies. Worker ants are sterile females who forage for food as their primary responsibility. Male ants exist for the sole purpose of reproduction and die soon after the mating swarm. The fertilized females establish colonies.

During red harvester ant mating swarms, winged males and females emerge from their colonies. They are attracted to each other by pheromones. After mating, the mated females shed their wings and establish new nesting sites. One colony can live up to 20 years.

Red harvester ant mating swarms occur annually in warm environments and at elevated heights. Red harvester ants are most active in temperatures of 35 to 40°C, and mating swarms typically occur in the afternoon after rainfall or heavy storms. In the United States, winged reproductive adults are seen throughout May, while mating flights begin in June. Although mating swarms occur between June and October, they are most common in the months of August and September. Red harvester ant mating swarms take place within a single day.

The swarming behavior of red harvester ants is commonly synchronized with nearby colonies. For this reason, it is common to witness large numbers of winged ants appearing in one area. Red harvester ants participate in "hill-topping," gathering around prominent points within a landscape–such as tall trees, chimneys and towers–while searching for mates. The U.S. West Tower in Denver is a famous hill-topping location for red harvester ants: millions of ants congregate in this area each year.

While red harvester ants are known to dwell primarily outdoors, winged ants can infest homes during swarming periods.

FLORIDA HARVESTER ANT

Scientific name: *Pogonomyrmex badius* (Latreille) (Insecta: Hymenoptera: Formicidae)

Introduction

Although the Florida harvester ant, *Pogonomyrmex badius* (Latreille), occurs throughout most of Florida it is limited by its ecological requirements. Where it does occur, the ant nest is readily visible as a large cleared area with a number of slow moving individuals on the surface near the nest. Harvester ants in the genus *Pogonomyrmex* received this name due to their practice of gathering seeds for food. While there are 22 species of harvester ants found in the United States, only the Florida harvester ant occurs east of the Mississippi River.

Distribution

The Florida harvester ant is found from Florida to North Carolina and west into Mississippi and Louisiana. The ant is the only eastern representative of the genus *Pogonomyrmex* .

Description

The adults are dark rust red in color (Haack and Granovsky 1990), with the worker caste strongly polymorphic (1/4 to 3/8 inch long). The major worker has a disproportionally enlarged head.

Like most other *Pogonomyrmex* spp. the Florida harvester ant has a psammophore (rows of long hair on ventral side of head) but it is poorly developed (Smith and Whitman 1992). The antennae are clubless with twelve segments. The thoracic dorsum has the sutures obsolescent or absent, and the thorax is not impressed between the masonotum and epinotum; The

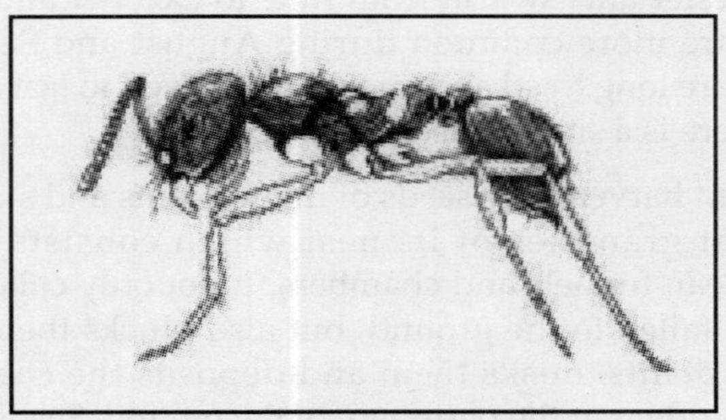

Worker

abdominal pedicel consists of two segments. The tibial spurs on the middle and hind legs are very finely pectinate.

Biology

The Florida harvester ant differs from all other *Pogonomyrmex* spp. in having polymorphic (more than one size) workers. The huge headed soldiers (major workers) are not abundant in the colonies and seem to be no more aggressive or pugnacious than the intermediate and smaller workers.

The Florida harvester ant nests exclusively or by preference in sand. It requires open areas in which to build its nest and tends to nest in open woodlands or grassy areas. Xeric hammocks are preferred. Many nests are found on lawns, around gardens, and in fire lanes. The mound is very slight and flattened with single or multiple entrances in the center and is from 30 to 60 cm in diameter. Unlike most other harvester ant species (Haack and Granovsky 1990), Florida harvester ant workers make no effort to clear vegetation from around the mound. However, the mound is often covered with small pebbles or charcoal from burned areas.

The ant is vigorously active in rather low relative humidity (below 55 percent) and in high temperatures (35-40°C). Mating swarms usually occur in the afternoon after a rain. Winged forms (reproductive adults) have been observed in the nests in May, and mating flights were recorded for June. Scientists state that harvester ants swarm from June to October although the swarms are more common during August and September. Colonies are long lived and one was observed to last at least 19 years. There is a single queen in each colony.

The ant harvests the seeds of many plants and stores them in the flat graneries of its nest which consists of many subterranean tunnels and chambers. It not only collects seeds that have fallen to the ground, but also plucks them directly from the plants, husks them and deposits the chaff on the kitchen middens at the periphery of the mound. Seeds from the following plants have been identified from nests: ragweed, crab grass, small crab grass, rough buttonweed, sedge, *Paspalium* sp., poke weed, red clover, alfalfa, evening primrose, narrow leaf vetch and crotonweed.

The Florida harvester ant moves its nest periodically (an average of once every 234 days) in response to changes in microclimate resulting from shading due to overhanging vegetation. *Pogonomyrmex* workers of one colony will readily fight members of another colony of the same or different ant species and continued strife of this kind also results in colony movement.

Economic Importance

The Florida harvester ant is not of economic importance to growers and homeowners, is not aggressive and almost has to be forced to sting someone. However, the sting is among the more painful of those received from ants and the pain lasts longer than usual for ant stings due to the poison injected. Some swelling may also occur as the reaction to their stings spread along the lymph channels.

Several ants stung me on the wrist, and after a few minutes an intense fiery pain began in this area which was about two inches in diameter. It turned deep red in color and immediately a watery, sticky secretion came out of the skin. This area became hot and feverish and the excruciating pain lasted all day and up into the night. At least one death, a child in Oklahoma, has been credited to stings by the red harvester ant, *P. barbatus*.

Management

Generally, management of the Florida harvester ant isn't necessary unless the ant is located where small children may be playing or in other similar circumstances. An adult may easily avoid the ant, thus avoiding the extremely painful sting. The Florida harvester ant uses odor trials as well as sun orientation to return to food sources so placing baits on these trails may help control a colony. Mounds should be treated during the hottest part of the day, as the ants are least active at this time, by injecting a labeled insecticidal dust into the entrance. Insect growth regulators are also recommended, but take longer to destroy the colony.

Red harvester ants are native species and are generally not considered to be serious pests. Consider the option of not controlling these ants, especially in areas inhabited by the few remaining horned lizards.

10

Leafcutter Ant

Scientific Classification

Kingdom	:	Animalia
Phylum	:	Arthropoda
Class	:	Insecta
Order	:	Hymenoptera
Family	:	Formicidae
Genus	:	Atta and Acromymex
Species	:	40 species

Leafcutter ants, a non-generic name, are any of 47 species of leaf-chewing ants belonging to the two genera *Atta* and *Acromyrmex*. These species of tropical, fungus-growing ants are all endemic to South and Central America, Mexico and parts of the southern United States. Leafcutter ants "cut and process fresh vegetation (leaves, flowers, and grasses) to serve as the nutritional substrate for their fungal cultivars."

The *Acromyrmex* and *Atta* ants have much in common anatomically; however, the two can be identified by their external differences. *Atta* ants have three pairs of spines and a smooth exoskeleton on the upper surface of the thorax, while *Acromyrmex* ants have four pairs and a rough exoskeleton.

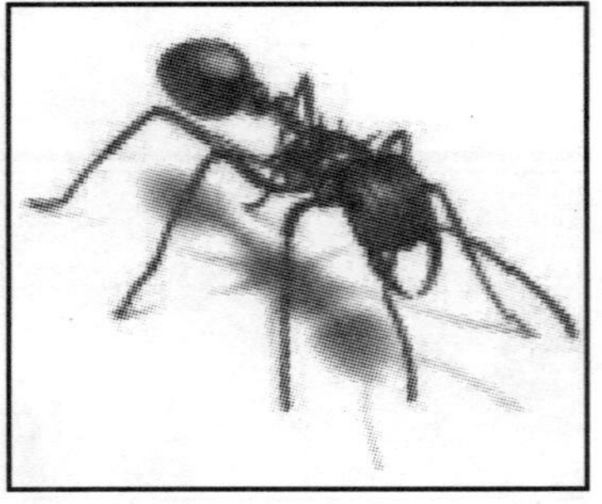

Next to humans, leafcutter ants form the largest and most complex animal societies on Earth. In a few years, the central mound of their underground nests can grow to more than 30 metres (98 ft) across, with smaller, radiating mounds extending out to a radius of 80 metres (260 ft), taking up 30 to 600 square metres (320 to 6,500 sq ft) and containing eight million individuals.

Leaf-cutter ants are very important to the ecology of the forests where they are found. Their fungus gardens help to make tropical soils more fertile. As the gardens grow, fertile soil usually only on the surface, is carried deeper into the ground, and the excavated soil, rich in mineral salts, is carried to the surface. However, due to the large amount of vegetation they consume, including crops, humans see them as pests. To try and get rid of them, people use slow-acting pesticides. These are carried back to the nest by the ants and will eventually kill all the individuals in the colony, including the Queen. These pesticides stay in the forest ecosystem for a long time, and cause considerable environmental damage.

Diet

Leafcutter Ants cut pieces of leaves or grass with strong jaws, then use the plant matter to grow their own fungus which they eat.

Habitat

About 39 species of Leaf-cutter ant have been identified. They are found in tropical regions of Central and South America.

Colony Life Cycle

Reproduction and Colony Founding

Winged females and males leave their respective nests *en masse* and engage in a nuptial flight known as the *revoada*. Each female mates with multiple males to collect the 300 million sperm she needs to set up a colony.

Once on the ground, the female loses her wings and searches for a suitable underground lair in which to found her colony. The success rate of these young queens is very low, and only 2.5% will go on to establish a long-lived colony. To start her own fungus garden, the queen stores bits of the parental fungus garden mycelium in her infrabuccal pocket, which is located within her oral cavity.The Queen usually only produces female offspring. However, when the colony is mature, she will produce both males and females which themselves will be able to reproduce. These individuals, about 40,000 males and up to 7,000 females, have wings, and fly out of the nest to a given height where they mate. After mating, each female sheds her wings, digs a chamber in the soil, and deposits the wad of fungus she has been carrying from her previous nest. She fertilises this, cultivates a new fungus garden, and lays her eggs. About three months later, the first workers emerge, and the new colony starts to grow. However, because they are vulnerable when flying, and there are no soldiers to protect the nest initially, very few Queens survive their first year.

Colony Hierarchy

In a mature leafcutter colony, ants are divided into castes, based mostly on size, that perform different functions. *Acromyrmex* and *Atta* exhibit a high degree of biological polymorphism, four castes being present in established colonies - minims, minors, mediae and majors. Majors are also known as soldiers or dinergates. *Atta* ants are more polymorphic than *Acromyrmex*, meaning there is comparatively less difference in size from the smallest to largest types of *Acromymex*.

- Minims are the smallest workers, and tend to the growing brood or care for the fungus gardens. Head width is less than 1 mm.
- Minors are slightly larger than minima workers, and are present in large numbers in and around foraging columns. These ants are the first line of defense and continuously patrol the surrounding terrain and vigorously attack any enemies that threaten the foraging lines. Head width is around 1.8-2.2 mm.
- Mediae are the generalized foragers, which cut leaves and bring the leaf fragments back to the nest.
- Majors, the largest worker ants, act as soldiers, defending the nest from intruders, although recent evidence indicates majors participate in other activities, such as clearing the main foraging trails of large debris and carrying bulky items back to the nest. The largest soldiers (*Atta laevigata*) may have total body lengths up to 16 mm and head widths of 7 mm.

Ant-fungus Mutualism

Their societies are based on an ant-fungus mutualism, and different species of ants use different species of fungus, but all of the fungi the ants use are members of the Lepiotaceae family. The ants actively cultivate their fungus, feeding it with freshly cut plant material and keeping it free from pests and molds. This mutualistic relationship is further augmented by another symbiotic partner; a bacterium that grows on the ants and secretes chemicals, - essentially the ants use portable antimicrobials. Leaf cutter ants are sensitive enough to adapt to the fungi's reaction to different plant material, apparently detecting chemical signals from the fungus. If a particular type of leaf is toxic to the fungus, the colony will no longer collect it. The only two other groups of insects to use fungus-based agriculture are ambrosia beetles and termites. The fungus cultivated by the adults is used to feed the ant larvae, and the adult ants feed off the leaf sap. The fungus needs the ants to stay alive, and the larvae need the fungus to stay alive.

Waste management

Leaf-cutter ants have very specific roles when it comes to taking care of the fungal garden and dumping the refuse. Waste management is a key role for each colony's longevity. The necrotrophic parasite *Escovopsis* of the fungal cultivar threatens the ants' food source, and is thus a constant danger to the ants. The waste-transporters and waste heap workers are the older, more dispensable leaf-cutter ants, ensuring the healthier and younger leaf-cutter ants can work on the fungal garden. The *Atta colombica* species, unusually for the *Attine* tribe, have an external waste heap. Waste-transporters take the waste, which consists of used substrate and discarded fungus, to the waste heap. Once dropped off at the refuse dump, heap-workers organise the waste and constantly shuffle it around to aid decomposition. A compelling observation of *Atta colombica* was that the dead ants were placed around the perimeter of the waste heap.

In addition to feeding the fungal garden with foraged food, mainly consisting of leaves, it is protected from *Escovopsis* by the antibiotic secretions of *Actinobacteria* (genus *Pseudonocardia*). This mutualistic micro-organism lives in the metapleural glands of the ant. *Actinobacteria* are responsible for producing the majority of the world's antibiotics today.

Parasitism

When the ants are out collecting leaves, they are at risk of being attacked by the phorid fly, a parasitic pest which lays eggs into the crevices of the worker ants' heads. Often a minim will sit on the worker ant and ward off any attack. Also, the wrong type of fungus can grow during cultivation. *Escovopsis* is a highly virulent fungus that has the potential to devastate an ant garden, as it is horizontally transmitted. Scientists found

Escovopsis was cultured, during colony foundation, in 6.6% of colonies. However, in one to two year old colonies, almost 60% had *Escovopsis* growing in the fungal garden.

Interactions with Humans

In some parts of their range, leafcutter ants can be quite a nuisance to humans, defoliating crops and damaging roads and farmland with their nest-making activities. For example, some *Atta* species are capable of defoliating an entire citrus tree in less than 24 hours. Deterring the leafcutter ant *Acromyrmex lobicornis* from defoliating crops has been found simpler than first expected. Collecting the refuse from the nest and placing it over seedlings or around crops resulted in a deterrent effect over a period of 30 days.

Leafcutter Ants Grow Fungus Cultures for Food

Leaf cutter ants grow their fungus cultures on a substrate made of ground up plant matter, which they obtain by harvesting prodigious amounts of leaves, petals, and various other plant parts from the vegetation surrounding the nest. When an ant scout finds a suitable bush or tree, it lays a scent trail back to the nest and summons the foragers. These medium sized ants (head widths of around 2 mm) cut out pieces of leaves and head clumsily back to the nest. All around them smaller ants weave to and fro, constantly scanning the surrounding terrain for danger. Some of these smaller ants may also hitchhike on the leaf fragments carried by their bigger sisters, although the function of this behavior is still unclear. One hypothesis is that the small ants are protecting their burdened comrades from tiny phorid flies that might lay eggs on the heads of the ants (the eggs hatch later and the growing larvae basically eat the heads of the unfortunate ants).

Once in awhile an observer can spot a large soldier as she gingerly steps over her rushing nestmates. These gigantic ants in some *Atta* species can have headwidths greater than 7 mm and total body lengths of more than 1.7 cm! Soldiers were generally thought to be highly specialized for defence, but new studies and observations have shown that soldiers in some species serve a variety of other functions.

When the foragers get to the nest, they hand the leaves to smaller ants, who rush it to one of the many culture gardens. The leaves are then processed into smaller and smaller fragments by smaller and smaller ants, until the thoroughly masticated result is placed into the growing culture. These fluffy-looking fungus cultures are tended by the tiniest ants, who roam inside the numerous galleries that ramify throughout the culture and harvest special nutritional bodies produced by the fungi called "gongylidia". These tiny ants then distribute their bounty to the rest of the colony (although most of the harvested nutritional bodies are fed to the ant larvae).

In order to protect their fungus cultures and combat invading fungi pests, these ants employ antibiotics produced by a *Streptomyces* bacteria that lives on their skin, in addition to physically removing the invading fungi. This interaction between ant, bacteria, and fingus crop is one of the most intricate examples of mutualism in nature!

The Leafcutter Caste System

The caste system in the *Atta* ants is one reason why these ants are so successful. Individual ants are specialized for various colony tasks based on their size and form. The queen is the reproductive female of the colony and is responsible for laying more eggs and increasing the colony population, while the workers (all non-reproductive females) can be divided into various subcastes, each with her own function. Younger workers, even the largest soldiers, remain inside the nest and do in-house tasks until they mature, but a worker's specialized function reveals itself sooner or later.

The smallest workers tend to the growing brood, while other small workers (head width less than 1 mm) care for the fungus gardens. They are optimized for these tasks because of their smaller sizes - it wouldn't do to have a gigantic soldier bumbling around inside the tiny tunnels of the fungus cultures!

Slightly larger minima workers (or minims) are present in large numbers in and around foraging columns. These ants are the first line of defense because they continuously patrol the surrounding terrain and vigorously attack any enemies that threaten the foraging lines.

Workers with headwidths of around 1.8-2.2 mm are the generalized foragers, who cut leaves and bring the leaf fragments back to the nest. In fact, researchers have found that this exact head size is optimum for cutting the average leaf!

The largest workers (called soldiers or majors) are mostly used to fight off large predators, although they are also an intimidating force against marauding *Nomamyrmex* army ants. In addition, as noted above, soldiers may perform other minor activities, such as removing obstructions from the ant foraging trails and handling very large items.

Finally, winged reproductives are produced by mature colonies. The young queens and male drones are fated to fly off and mate with young queens and drones from other colonies to produce new leafcutter ant colonies. The males die soon after mating with several females, but the mortality rate among the potential queens is frighteningly high as well. Only a very small percentage of incipient leafcutter colonies reach their 3 year anniversary. Most young colonies probably die off when their fungus fails for one reason or another, while a few are overwhelmed by vertebrate and other predators.

The Founding of the Colony

Before flying off to start their new colonies, the virgin queens take some fungi culture with them. They will use these to start the new fungus garden. Like most other ant species, leafcutter ants engage in a "nuptial flight", whereby virgin queens and males from many colonies take flight at around the same time in order to mate. The flight capabilities of leafcutter queens are not well known, but *Atta texana* queens have been recorded to travel up to 10.5 km. After insemination by several males during the nuptial flight, the queens land and search for a likely spot to start their nest. Most leafcutter colonies are founded via haplometrosis (a single founding queen), however, pleometrosis has been seen in *A. texana* and *Acromyrmex versicolor*. For awhile, the new queen has to depend on trophic eggs and muscle catalysis in order to survive, but once she has reared the first brood, the small workers can start foraging and enlarge the fungus garden.

Atta mother queens during colony founding demonstrate the most complex behavior among dealate female ants, mostly because the female has to not only rear her first brood of workers, but she also has to rear the fungus on which the future of the colony depends. The weight of dealate *Atta* queens varies from species to species, but all *Atta* queens are huge (*Acromyrmex* queens are much smaller), exceeded in size only by the grotesque queens of doryline driver ants. The table below from Mintzer (1990) shows some weights for dealate females:

Species	Initial weights (mg)
Atta texana	300-400 mg
Atta cephalotes	500-600 mg
Atta sexdens rubropilosa	400-500 mg
Atta capiguara	up to 800 mg or more

All females lose weight during colony foundation before the first workers appear, typically 30-35% for *Atta mexicana* and *Atta texana* and 17-39% for the larger *Atta cephalotes*. This is because the female has to use up her energy reserves to rear the new workers and fungus without outside foraging.

The future mother queen is tireless in taking care of her larval brood and fungus. She cultures the growing mat of fungus (which develops as a disk or mat of mycelium) on her own fecal fluid, and feeds the first larval brood her own eggs.

It takes 35-38 days for the first workers to emerge from their pupae in Atta texana and Atta cephalotes, and these new ants are relatively small (2-4 mm total body lengths for *Atta texana* and *Atta mexicana*, although some *Atta cephalotes* first brood workers were larger - up to 5.5 mm). Once the first workers develop and start to forage on the outside, they take over all the duties of the queen, which thereafter retires into a life of egg-laying.

Cofoundresses of *Acromyrmex versicolor* display an interesting and unusual behavior, where one of the unrelated co-founding queens becomes a foraging specialist, and takes all the risks of foraging above-ground for the group. The queen assigned to do this hazardous job is seemingly not picked based on size or reproductive capabilities (as measured by ovary size). In cases where the assigned queen refuses to do her job, the entire group usually is doomed since the group delays or does not replace the specialist forager, and the fungus garden dies.

The path to maturity for a young nest is fraught with peril at every turn. Predation on queens both during the nuptial flight and after landing is very high. Birds, armadillos, rodents, and especially other ants prey heavily on the plump and juicy female reproductives. Even after workers emerge and the colony starts growing quickly, survivorship of these incipient colonies is very low. One study found that only 2.5% of young *A. sexdens* colonies were still alive after three months. Excluding major predators like armadillos, rodents, and other ants still resulted in very low survivorship, with at most 1.9-6.4% of the colonies surviving after three months. Thus, most deaths of young colonies are probably due to the failure of the fungus garden, the spread of pathogens, or even because the queen was not fertilized.

The Leafcutter Nests

The leafcutter nests, especially of the *Atta* spp, are marvels of engineering. Young colonies typically have only a few nest mounds, with foraging holes opening several meters away from the mounds, but the numerous (up to hundreds of nest openings) nest mounds of large mature colonies sometimes fuse together to form one huge mound. In this case, the central nest mound may be 30 m in diameter, have numerous 0.3 m diameter feeder mounds extending outwards to a radius of 80 m, and may occupy 30 to 600 square meters! More amazing, the underground chambers may extend downwards to more than six meters in depth!

The immense size of Atta nests, and the very large populations of the colony, can cause problems in terms of creating enough ventilation throughout the nest to prevent the high build-up of CO_2 and loss of oxygen. There are two mechnisms by which leafcutter ants may prevent from suffocating.

In the first method, called thermal convection, the hundreds of nest openings in mature Atta nests create a ventilation system that continuously circulates air throughout the nest. Because the central chambers tend to have the brood chambers and gardens, these areas become somewhat warmer than the peripheral chambers. The warm air moves up and out through the central hole openings, drawing colder air from the outer chambers into the central area. This in turn draws fresh air from the outside into the nest holes on the periphery.

The second method is called wind-induced ventilation, and this was elucidated by the researchers. In this case, air is drawn out of the central nest mound openings by wind blowing over the nest openings. This outflow in turn causes air to rush into the nest via the outlying nest holes and tunnels, thus ensuring the rapid circulation of air throughout the nest chambers.

Leafcutter ant Waste Management Systems

Because of the peculiarities of their fungus-growing lifestyle, leafcutter ants may have one of the most sophisticated waste management systems in nature. Like human cities, leafcutter nests produce copious amounts of waste product (including spent fungal substrate, dead ants, and the like), which could cause diseases not only in the ants, but in their fungus cultures.

The first line of defence is the deliberate segregation of waste products away from the main nest chambers. These "dump" or waste "heap" areas may be internal in some species (for example, *A. cephalotes* has large dump chambers situated on the nest periphery), or it may be located in external piles away from the nest mounds (in *A. mexicana* and *A. colombica*, the waste dumps may reach a meter of more in height in large colonies!).

The second line of defence is the creation of "waste workers" who specialize in working constantly with the waste. These ants can be separated into two groups: (1) transporters who carry waste products from the sources and unload them close to, or at the periphery of, the waste dump; and (2) heap workers who live exclusively in the waste heap and work to aerate and turn it over constantly. The second type in particular is strongly ostracized from the nest proper by other colony members, who may kill them if they persist in trying to venture too far away from the heap.

The third line of defense is behavioural, with the overall aim always being to minimize exposure of the main nest and workers to any waste products. For example, researchers found that in *A. colombica* (which has external dumps), the location of the waste heaps in large colonies is influenced by the environment, such that heaps are placed lower than the nest mounds if there is a slope. The result of this is that no waste matter will be inadvertantly introduced into the mounds during rainstorms. In addition, foraging lines always bypass the heap area.

Through these methods, leafcutter ants ensure the continued health of the colony and its fungus culture.

Leafcutter Ants and Human Beings

Leafcutter ants have benefitted greatly from the spread of humanity. Nest densities of some of the leafcutters reach very high levels in man-made areas, including urbanized locations such as small towns and cities. Because of the ubiquity and ecological dominance of leafcutters, local people in the areas where they are present recognize and know these types of ants, and are able to distinguish them easily from the many other ants.

The dominance of leafcutters in urban areas may be due to several factors:

Firstly, many leafcutter species seem to be adapted for open areas, so the destruction of primary and secondary forests by man has opened up new land for the exploitation of these ants.

Secondly, whereas leafcutters do well even in highly urbanized locations (e.g. there were some large leafcutter nests in the middle of downtown San Jose, Costa Rica), the few predators that can breach their nest defences (some vertebrates(?), *Nomamyrmex* army ants) are not as adaptable and are almost wholly absent in these areas.

Thirdly, ants which deterred predation on certain plants (e.g. *Azteca* ants nesting in Cecropia trees) may not exist in urbanized and other man-created habitats, thus allowing leafcutters to exploit these new food sources.

Finally, the presence of human beings has altered the biological landscape to a degree that is favorable for leafcutters. For example, many of the exotic and crop plants favored by humans are entirely deficient in the protective defenses of native trees and plants in the local region.

The economic impact of leafcutter ants on people is quite pronounced. Each leafcutter colony can consume as much leaf matter in a day as a full grown cow, and leafcutter ants are by far the dominant "herbivores" in the neotropics, with the amount of vegetable matter being cut estimated at an astonishing 12-17% of annual leaf production! Damage (indirect and direct) has been estimated to be in the billions (USA dollars) annually, and the grass cutting species reduces the carrying capacity of pasturelands in the area by as much as 10%!

Controlling Leafcutter Ants

Leafcutter ants are extremely fascinating critters, but they do become pests when they start carting off plants from your garden or farm.

Physical Deterrents

People can protect their trees and plants by physically preventing the ants from getting to them. One method is to place plastic skirts around the area, and coat these with sap or long-lasting adhesives. Another method people have used is to create moat barriers around their gardens and plants by digging a bamboo or platic-lined trench around the area and then filling this with soapy water.

Chemical Deterrents

The following methods have been used with varying success to prevent leafcutters from encroaching on valuable gardens.

- Use lime to coat barriers. I have seen this used extensively in Mexico, where the white rings of lime are painted near the base of trees to prevent the omnipresent leafcutters from scaling the trees.
- Use Basil Oil extracts to coat barriers.
- Plant lemon grass and other plants that repel leafcutters around your garden.
- Use garlic sprays to repel ants.
- Use waste and soil from another leafcutter colony to surround your plants. Because leafcutter ants are territorial, foragers encountering soil from another leafcutter nest may avoid it.

Other Chemicals

Treat nests with:

- Diatomaceous earth - an inorganic substance that is abrasive to insects and causes them to dessicate)
- Pyrethrum - a botanical insecticide

11

Marauder Ant

Scientific Classification

Kingdom	: Animalia
Phylum	: Arthropoda
Class	: Insecta
Order	: Hymenoptera
Family	: Formicidae
Subfamily	: Myrmicinae
Tribe	: Solenopsidini
Genus	: Pheidologeton Mayr, 1862
Species	: *P. affinis, P. diversus, P. hostilis, P. melanocephalus, P. pygmaeus, P. silenus, many more.*
Diversity	: c. 40 species

Pheidologeton is a genus of ants, also called marauder ants, due to their raids similar to those of army ants. Their nests are more permanent but almost as large as those of army ants. This genus of ant is recognisable by its dramatic polymorphism, the difference in sizes of the worker castes; there is a super-major worker in addition to major and minor.

There are about 42 species/subspecies in this genus. They range from Africa through south Asia into Australia.

Two fossil species are known.

Habitat

Pheidologeton ants are predaceous insects of the African, Asian, and Australian tropics that form massive colonies. Some species conduct raids similar to those of the nomadic army ants, although marauder ants have more permanent nests in the soil. Worker polymorphism is well-developed in *Pheidologeton*, supermajor workers are much larger than the majors and tiny minors.

The most notable thing about these ants is the large variation in the size of the workers. The smallest can measure only 2.0 to 2.5 mm while the largest super majors can be nearly 20 mm. There are also many intermediate forms between these sizes. The difference in size between the minor and major workers is said to be the greatest of all ant species.

The smaller workers do most of the work in the colony and take care of the brood and queen. They are also found outside the nest in large numbers on the hunting trails. The larger major workers are found in the nest acting as guards and food storage containers. They are also found outside on the trails where they use their powerful jaws to cut up the larger prey into more manageable pieces – so it can be carried away by the smaller workers.

This species hunts its food by sending out thousands of workers on long 'swarm trails' which are used for several days to collect anything edible nearby. In their natural habitat they prefer to forage from early evening to late morning to avoid the mid-day heat.

The individual ants are very aggressive and do not retreat when challenged. They do not sting but give painful bites. The smaller workers are much more aggressive than the larger majors and will swarm over any potential food, however if the larger major workers fasten their powerful jaws onto you their bite can be extremely painful.

Diet

They feed on a wide range of foods and seem to accept almost anything including seeds, meats and sugary excretions. In the dry season when other food is scarce large amounts of seeds are collected. Large prey or excess food and often the trails themselves are frequently concealed with earthen covers, probably to help protect the ants and their food from other predators.

The queens are slightly larger than the largest majors at about 20-25 mm. The alates are active at dusk and the males are too large for the females to carry so mating occurs on the ground. When a male encounters a female he 'buzzes' her with her wings making an audible sound and quickly mates with her. Females will copulate with several males. The newly fertilized females are quite capable of starting their own colonies independently, but often after their nuptial flight a few will return to their original nest and bud off with a mass of workers forming an instant colony.

Nesting

In the nest the fertile queens are constantly guarded and groomed by the small workers - and if a colony is disturbed the workers will rush to the queen and completely cover her presenting any potential predator with a seething mass of biting ants. Often in observation nests when you are looking for the queen all you can see is a swirling mass of small workers moving around all over where she is.

Some colonies especially those in their early years will only contain a single queen, but older nests - located in prime locations and where they have unlimited food, will often accept several queens back into the colony and form multi queen colonies. Such colonies can grow to very large sizes and are very difficult to observe close up. The ants sense anyone approaching the nest site probably by ground vibrations and send out a mass of workers in defense - rendering it very difficult to stay near the nest for all but a brief time.

They are vigorous excavators but also will often use burrows of other insects and small animals to construct a deeper nest. Wild nests can often extend to 60 cm plus into the ground. This may not seem very deep but taking into consideration that the smaller workers are only 2mm it's quite an achievement.

Due to the size of the colonies in time they frequently consume all resources in a particular area and they will then move their whole nest. This is usually done at night over a period of several days. There new nest locations can be significant distances from the old nests – one I followed from a flooded rice field was relocating over fifty meters away.

In the wild they are attracted to moist places where more potential prey can usually be found and where trails can easily be covered with earthen defenses. In dry seasons they will frequently appear near irrigated farmland and near houses after gardens have been watered.

12

Odorous House Ant

This ant gets its name from the strong, rotten coconut-like smells it gives off when crushed and the fact that they commonly nest in or around houses. Native to the United States, these ants are very social, living in colonies of up to 100,000 members.

Tapinoma sessile is a species of ant that goes by the common names odorous house ant, stink ant, and coconut ant.

Scientific Classification

Common Name	:	Odorous House Ant
Kingdom	:	Animalia
Phylum	:	Arthropoda
Class	:	Insecta
Order	:	Hymenoptera
Family	:	Formicidae
Species	:	*Tapinoma sessile*

Description

Size	:	1/16"to 1/8"
Shape	:	Segmented, Oval

Colour : Brown or Black

Legs : 6

Wings : Varies

Antenna : Yes

Tapinoma sessile (Say), the odorous house ant, is a widely distributed native species found throughout the United States, in Canada, and Mexico. The common name of this insect is derived from a peculiar coconutlike odor produced in the anal glands. Large populations of these ants live in western Washington, between Vancouver, British Columbia and Portland, Oregon. Odorous house ants are less common in the semidesert areas of the Pacific Northwest.

Identification

All odorous house ant workers are the same size (monomorphic). They differ from other ant species by the presence of a slit-like cloacal orifice without fringe hairs (Fig. 12.1). The antennae have 12 segments without a club (enlargement) at the tip. The promesonotal and mesoepinotal sutures are both distinct; the latter is even more distinct. The singlesegmented petiole (connection between thorax and abdomen) has no node.

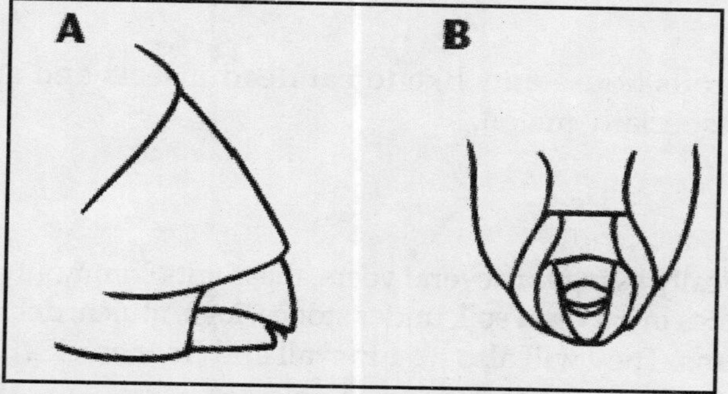

Fig. 12.1. Transverse ventral orifice (A. lateral view, B. ventral view).

Biology

Odorous house ants have adapted to a wide range of habitats and thrive nearly everywhere from sea level to about 10,500 feet. They nest in sand, pastures, grass fields, forests, bogs, and houses, frequently under stones and logs. They also build nests under stumps and the bark of dead trees, in bird and mammal nests, plant galls, and debris. Nests in soil are shapeless, shallow, and temporary, as the ants frequently move. Colonies can consist of thousands of workers and usually contain many queens.

New queens typically mate with their brothers within the colony. Some queens also mate with unrelated males. Nuptial flights occur only outside colonies, from June to mid-July. New colonies may form by budding when a new queen(s) leaves the parent colony with workers or as a single foundress queen. Workers move fast and often travel in columns. When alarmed they run about erratically with abdomens tipped while releasing an alarm pheromone (the peculiar coconut-like odor), which draws more workers to the release site.

Workers collect honeydew excretions from mealybugs, aphids, scale insects, and plant hoppers and will protect these insects from predators. Workers also gather nectar from plants and feed on both living and dead insects.

Diet

Odorous house ants like to eat dead insects and sugary sweets, especially melon.

Habitat

Typically living for several years, these ants commonly make their homes in exposed soil, under stones, logs, mulch, debris and other items. They will also nest in wall and floor cracks.

Behaviour

- Feed on both dead and living insects, favoring aphid and scale honeydew
- In homes, forage primarily for sweets
- Travel in both wandering patterns and set trails
- Trails common along branches of trees, foundations, sidewalks, baseboards, and edges of carpets
- When disturbed, become erratic with their abdomens raised in the air

Nest type and size

- Live in shallow nests in soil under stones, wood, or debris
- May nest in various habitats including wooded areas, beaches, wall voids, and around water pipes and heaters
- Large colonies, with up to 10,000 workers and many queens

Impact

Odorous House ants do not pose a health threat, but they can contaminate food by leaving waste behind.

Prevention

- Avoid using other individuals' combs, hats, towels, etc.
- Eliminate standing water. Pests, such as ants, mosquitoes and termites, are attracted to moisture.
- Keep tree branches and other plants cut back from the house. Sometimes pests use these branches to get into your home.

13

Pavement Ant

Scientific Classification

Kingdom	:	Animalia
Phylum	:	Arthropoda
Class	:	Insecta
Order	:	Hymenoptera
Family	:	Formicidae
Subfamily	:	Myrmicinae
Genus	:	Tetramorium
Species	:	T. caespitum
Binomial name	:	*Tetramorium caespitum* (Linnaeus, 1758

The pavement ant, *Tetramorium caespitum,* is a common household pest. Its name comes from the fact that colonies usually make their homes in pavement. It is distinguished by one spine on the back, two nodes on the petiole, and grooves on the head and thorax. The species is native to Europe, but was introduced to North America in the 18th century.

During early spring, colonies attempt to conquer new areas and often attack nearby enemy colonies. These result in huge sidewalk battles, sometimes leaving thousands of ants dead. Because of their aggressive nature, they often invade and colonize seemingly impenetrable areas. In summer time the

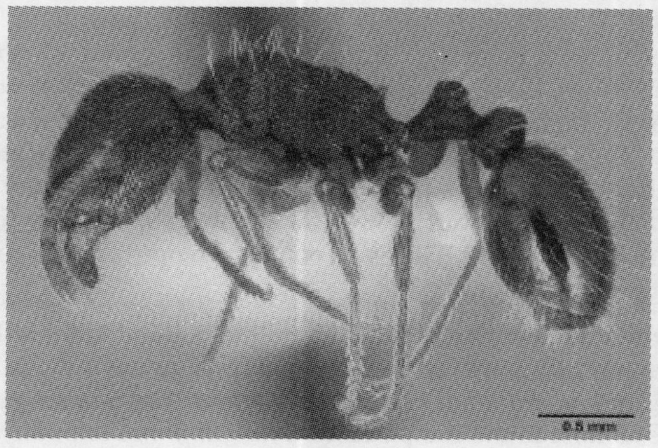

ants dig out the sand in between the pavements to vent the nests.

Although these ants can live inside, they get their name because they make their nests in or under cracks in pavement. They are typically found in the eastern half of the United States, California and Washington. Pavement ant colonies average 3,000 to 4,000 members and have several queens.

Description

Size	:	1/8"
Shape	:	Segmented, Oval
Colour	:	Dark Brown to Black
Legs	:	6
Wings	:	Varies
Antenna	:	Yes

The pavement ant is dark brown to blackish, and 2.5–4 mm long. Like other ants there are the workers, alates, and a queen. Alates, or new queen ants and drones, have wings, and are twice as large as the workers.

The drone's only job is to mate with the queen, and reproduction is at its highest in spring and summer. Tetramorium, like many other ants have nuptial flights where drones fly high up in the air and mate with new queens. The queen finds a suitable nesting location and digs a founding chamber. As the eggs hatch and the ants develop they will spend that time, about two to three months, tending to the queen of their colony. They will continue helping in the colony until they are a month old.

Older workers hunt and defend the colony. They will eat almost anything, including insects, seeds, honeydew, honey, bread, meats, nuts, ice cream and cheese. The pavement ant serves as host to the ectoparasitic *Teleutomyrmex schneideri.*

Life History

Very little information is available on pavement ant colony biology. Most information is gleaned from the observations of ant behavior aboveground.

Winged reproductive ants typically swarm in the spring but have been known to emerge any time of the year in heated structures. It is not uncommon to see swarming in late fall and into February even in colder climates.

After emergence, the ants mate and the queens burrow into the soil to begin laying eggs. Worker ants develop over a two-to-three-month period.

Most colonies are located under sidewalks, building slabs, and large rocks. Ants enter buildings through cracks in foundation walls and interior slabs. It is common to see sand piles and small soil particles in structures near cracks in concrete slabs or at the top of foundation walls where the ants deposit debris from excavated nests. Similar piles are seen in the warmer months at the cracks in sidewalks.

Pavement ants feed on a wide variety of food. Sweets, including sugar, nectar, fruits, and syrups are readily taken.

Grease, dead insects, and small seeds also are collected and stored in the nest. Nearly any morsel of food that falls to the floor will be consumed.

DIET

These ants will eat almost anything, including insects, grease, seeds, honeydew, honey, bread, meats, nuts and cheese.

HABITAT

This ant gets its name because it most commonly nests in soil next to and beneath slabs, sidewalks, patios, and driveways. Indoors, pavement ants nest under a building's foundation and within hollow foundation walls.

Colonization

When the pavement ants' colony is located outdoors, it can be easily found by the mound of soil over top the nest. This ant builds its colony beneath pavement, rocks, driveways, sidewalks, and logs. As it tunnels into the soil to excavate its colony, it pushes the soil debris up through the top of its nest, forming visible mounds of sandy-looking soil. These mounds are often seen between cracks of pavement, beneath which the ants have built their nest, thus the common name of "pavement" ant.

A typical colony will have 3,000 to 5,000 ants, but colonies have been known to grow as large as 30,000 ants at a single site. This is due, in part, to this ant's ability to have multiple queens in a single colony, whereas most ant species have only one queen per colony.

Ant Battles

The activity of this ant may be hard to detect, because it is most active at night. However, if you have neighboring pavement ant colonies, and you happen to be out at the right time, you just might witness the unique sight of an ant battle. In a fight for territory, these battles can leave hundreds of dead ants on the "battlefield."

Not a Termite

The pavement ant can cause concern when its winged "swarmers" emerge in the spring through mid-summer, as they are sometimes thought to be termites. However, pavement ants can be differentiated from termites by their:

- **Wings**: ants' front wings are longer than the back wings; termite wings are equal length.
- **Body**: ants have a narrow waist; the termite's thick waist gives it the appearance of having a single body part.
- **Antennae**: ants' antennae are elbowed; termites' are straight.
- **Size**: the pavement ant is much smaller than the termite.

Impact

Pavement ants do not pose a health threat, but they can contaminate food by leaving waste behind.

Prevention

- Eliminate standing water. Pests, such as ants, mosquitoes and termites, are attracted to moisture.
- Keep tree branches and other plants cut back from the house. Sometimes pests use these branches to get into your home.
- Make sure that there are no cracks or little openings around the bottom of your house. Sometimes pests use these to get into your home.
- Make sure that firewood and building materials are not stored next to your home. Pests like to build nests in stacks of wood.

14

Red Imported Fire Ants

Scientific Classification

Kingdom	:	Animalia
Phylum	:	Arthropoda
Class	:	Insecta
Order	:	Hymenoptera
Family	:	Formicidae
Subfamily	:	Myrmicinae
Tribe	:	Solenopsidini
Genus	:	Solenopsis
Species	:	S. invicta
Binomial name	:	*Solenopsis invicta* Buren, 1972
Synonyms	:	*Solenopsis saevissima wagneri* Santschi, 1916

Description

Size	:	1/8" to 3/8"
Shape	:	Segmented, Oval
Color	:	Dark Reddish Brown

Legs : 6

Wings : Varies

Antenna : Yes

The red imported fire ant (*Solenopsis invicta*), or simply RIFA, is one of over 280 species in the widespread genus *Solenopsis*. Although the red imported fire ant is native to South America, it has become a pest in the southern United States, Australia, Taiwan, Philippines, and the southern Chinese provinces of Guangdong, Guangxi, Fujian and Hong Kong. There are also reports of ant hills in Macau, the former Portuguese enclave that borders the province of Guangdong. RIFA are known to have a strong, painful, and persistent irritating sting that often leaves a pustule on the skin.

Red Imported Fire Ants are more aggressive than other ant species and have a painful sting. These ants and their telltale mound nests should be actively avoided. Red Imported Fire Ants can adapt to many climates and conditions in and around their environment. For example, if the colony senses increased water levels in their nests, they will come together and form a huge ball or raft that is able to float on the water!

RIFAs are more aggressive than most native ant species, and have a painful sting. An animal, including humans, typically encounters them by inadvertently stepping into one of their mounds, which causes the ants to swarm up the legs, attacking *en masse*. The ants respond to pheromones released by the first ant to attack and sting in concert, often killing smaller animals by overloading their immune systems.

Fire ants live in colonies that may have 100,000 to 500,000 ants. The queen of the colony can lay from 1500 to 5000 eggs per day, never leaves the nest and can live for many years. Worker ants take care of the queen and her eggs, build the nest, defend the colony, and find food. Preferred food of fire ants consists of protein-rich sources such as insects and seeds. Winged male and female ants fly from the colony in the spring and summer to mate in the air. The males die and the females become queens that start new colonies.

Only the red imported fire ant has a median clypeal tooth and a striated mesepimeron; these may be difficult to see at first. RIFA also have an antennal scape that nearly reaches the vertex, a post-petiole that is constricted at the back half, and the petiolar process is small or absent. Of the native fire ant species, the southern fire ant (*Solenopsis xyloni*) looks the most like the red imported fire ant. It can be identified by its brown to black color, well-developed petiolar process, and no median clypeal tooth. Desert fire ants (*Solenopsis aurea* and *S. amblychila*) are both yellowish-red to reddish-yellow and have a well-developed petiolar process. RIFA can also be identified by the proportion of large to small workers in disturbed mounds. If half the workers in disturbed mounds are large and dark, it is RIFA. If only a few large ants appear relative to hundreds of small ants, it is non-RIFA.

RIFAs compete successfully against other ants, and have been enlarging their range.

They are a pest, not only because of the physical pain they can inflict, but also because their mound-building activity can damage plant roots, lead to loss of crops, and interfere with mechanical cultivation. It is not uncommon for several fire ant mounds to appear suddenly in a suburban yard or a farmer's field, seemingly overnight. Their stings are rarely life-threatening to humans and other large animals, causing only 80 documented deaths as of 2006. However, they often kill smaller animals, such as birds. They sometimes kill newborn calves if they do not get on their feet quickly enough. The sting of the RIFA has venom composed of a necrotizing alkaloid, which causes both pain and the formation of white pustules that appear one day after the sting.

Fire ants are excellent natural predators and are biological controls for pests such as the sugarcane borer, the rice stink bug, the striped earwig, aphids, the boll weevil, the soybean looper, the cotton leafworm, the hornfly, and many other pests harmful to crops. However, they also kill beneficial pollinators, such as ground-nesting bee species. Seeds, fruits, leaves, roots, bark, nectar, sap, fungi, and carrion are all fire ant prey, and they are not shy about creating their own carrion, either. They are proficient enough at overwhelming intruders that they can virtually clear an area of invertebrates, lizards, and ground-dwelling birds.

Red imported fire ants are extremely resilient, and have adapted to contend with both flooding and drought conditions. If the ants sense increased water levels in their nests, they will come together and form a huge ball or raft that is able to float, with the workers on the outside and the queen inside. Once the ball hits a tree or other stationary object, the ants swarm onto it and wait for the water levels to recede. To contend with drought conditions, their nest structure includes a network of underground foraging tunnels that extends down to the water table. Also, although they do not hibernate during the winter, colonies can survive temperatures as low as 16 °F ("9 °C).

RIFAs were the first clearcut case discovered of a green-beard gene, by which natural selection can favor altruistic behavior.

Morphology

Red imported fire ants have both a pedicel and postpediole. In other words, they belong to a group of ants that have two humps between the thorax and abdomen. The workers have ten antennal segments terminating in a two-segmented club. It is often difficult to distinguish between the red imported fire ant *Solenopsis invicta* and some other species in the genus. A number of characters are used, but are not always consistent between the black imported fire ant (*Solenopsis richteri*) or hybrids between the two species. Positive identifications can be made using high performance liquid chromatography (HPLC) to distinguish differences in the cuticular hydrocarbons.

Diet

They primarily feed on vegetation.

Habitat

Red imported fire ants will build their nests in mounds of soil outdoors, in landscape areas or near a building's foundation. They occasionally enter buildings through holes or cracks in walls and foundations.

Impact

The sting of a Red Imported Fire Ant is painful and often results in a raised welt that becomes a white blister. Persons allergic to insect stings will react more severely. They are frustrating, not only because of the physical pain they can inflict, but because their mound-building activity can damage plant roots and lead to loss of crops.

PREVENTION

- Eliminate standing water. Pests, such as ants, mosquitoes and termites, are attracted to moisture.
- Keep tree branches and other plants cut back from the house. Sometimes pests use these branches to get into your home.
- Make sure that there are no cracks or little openings around the bottom of your house. Sometimes pests use these to get into your home.
- Make sure that firewood and building materials are not stored next to your home. Pests like to build nests in stacks of wood.

15

Weaver Ant

Scientific Classification

Kingdom	:	Animalia
Phylum	:	Arthropoda
Class	:	Insecta
Order	:	Hymenoptera
Family	:	Formicidae
Subfamily	:	Formicinae
Tribe	:	Oecophyllini
Genus	:	Oecophylla Smith, 1860

Species

†Oecophylla atavina, †Oecophylla bartoniana, †Oecophylla brischkei, †Oecophylla crassinoda, †Oecophylla eckfeldiana, †Oecophylla grandimandibula, †Oecophylla leakeyi, Oecophylla longinoda, †Oecophylla longiceps, †Oecophylla megarche, †Oecophylla obesa, †Oecophylla perdita, †Oecophylla praeclara, †Oecophylla sicula, Oecophylla smaragdina, †Oecophylla superba, †Oecophylla xiejiaheensis

Diversity Species

Oecophylla longinoda in blue,

Oecophylla smaragdina Fabricius, 1775 in red.

Weaver ants or Green ants (genus *Oecophylla*) are eusocial insects of the family Formicidae (order Hymenoptera). Weaver ants are obligately arboreal and are known for their unique nest building behaviour where workers construct nests by weaving together leaves using larval silk. Colonies can be extremely large consisting of more than a hundred nests spanning numerous trees and contain more than half a million workers. Like many other ant species, weaver ants prey on small insects and supplement their diet with carbohydrate-rich honeydew excreted by small insects (Hemiptera). *Oecophylla* workers exhibit a clear bimodal size distribution, with almost no overlap between the size of the minor and major workers. The major workers are approximately eight to ten millimeters in length and the minors approximately half the length of the majors. There is a division of labour associated with the size difference between workers. Major workers forage, defend, maintain and expand the colony whereas minor workers tend to stay within the nests where they care for the brood and 'milk' scale insects in or close to the nests. *Oecophylla* weaver ants vary in color from reddish to yellowish brown dependent on the species. *Oecophylla smaragdina* found in Australia often have bright green gasters. These ants are highly territorial and workers aggressively defend their territories against intruders. Because of their aggressive behaviour, weaver ants are sometime used by indigenous farmers, particularly in southeast Asia, as natural biocontrol agents against agricultural pests. Although *Oecophylla* weaver ants lack a functional sting they can inflict painful bites and often spray formic acid directly at the bite wound resulting in intense discomfort.

Weaver ants are best known for their remarkable nest construction. Using precise coordination, the weaver ants create very strong ant chains by linking legs to pull and bend leaves into desired tent like positions. The ants then use their own larvae to secrete a silk that is used to stitch leaves together to create a nest. They may have several nests dominating a few trees at once.

They are very aggressive territorial ants and for over 1000 years they have often been used by farmers to control agricultural pests.

Oecophylla smaragdina workers have a vice like grip and tremendous strength. A worker has been recorded to support 100 times its own weight whilst standing upside down on glass.

The life cycle

Weaver ants or Green ants (genus *Oecophylla*) are eusocial insects of the family Formicidae (order Hymenoptera).Weaver ants get their name from their habit of binding fresh leaves with silk to form their nests. Oecophylla weaver ants vary in color from reddish to yellowish brown dependent on the species. *Oecophylla smaragdina* found in Australia often have bright green gasters. In Vietnam they are called "ki¿n vàng" (yellow ants). The life cycle of the ant has four stages: egg, larva, pupa, and adult.

Eggs of weaver ants

The queen ant starts the ants' nests/colonies. She flies and searches for mate/s. She can mate with one or a few males (one at a time) in the air, or on low vegetation, or on the ground. Once mated, she looks for a nest site, either on trees or open fields. Once situated, she gets rid of her wings, seals herself into a small chamber and lays a small batch of eggs. The eggs then hatch into larvae. The queen is located in one nest and her eggs are distributed to all the other nests where workers and soldier ants are found. She spends her life laying eggs. The workers are females and do the work in the nest. The larger ones are the soldiers who defend their colony.

Fertilized eggs develop into females (workers and the queen) and unfertilized eggs into males. Female ants have 2 copies of each chromosome while males have one.

Larvae and Pupa of weaver ants

The larvae feed on the unfertilized eggs as food which the queen lays especially for them. The first brood of workers are normally smaller since she can only provide a limited amount of food. Once the ants mature, they leave the nest and begin to look for preys. They bring food to the queen and their siblings so that later offspring are bigger. As the colony reaches maturity, it begins to produce the queens and males for the next generation. Males can remain in the nests for some months and most of them will die within a few days after leaving their nests.

The larvae have special glands to produce lots of strong silks (adults do not produce silk). One colony is found over several nests that may be placed in various locations in a tree, or several trees, or in fields.

The worker ants form a chain along the edge of the leaf and pull the edges together by shortening the chain by one ant at a time. Once the leaf edges are in place, each ant holds one larva in its mandibles and gently squeezes the larva to produce silk. The silk is used to glue the leaf edges together.

Pupae are laid in nest with a short time before become adults.

Adult weaver ants

Adult weaver ants are reddish to brown in color and have 10-segmented antennae with 2-segmented clubs. Their eyes are relatively larger than those of other species of ants. They do not have stingers, but can give painful bites caused by the chemicals secreted from their abdomen. They make nests in trees or on leaves of legumes, or in bunds or levees of the fields. They have the most complex nests among ants' nests. They use fresh leaves to build nests .

Queen 20-25mm, a strong ant, normally green and brown, **monogyn** (one queen per colony).

Workers 5-6mm. Mostly orange. Sometimes this species has green **gasters.** Minor workers tend to look after the brood and farm scale bugs for honey dew.

Major workers 8-10mm. Mostly orange, this ant has long strong legs, long flexible **antennae** and large **mandibles.** These ants **forage**, maintain and expand the nest.

A dealate queen of *O. smaragdina* having shed her wings after a mating flight.

O. smaragdina major workers inspecting and cleaning (allogrooming) another worker on its return to the nest.

Their lifecycle spans a period of 8 to 10 weeks.

Distribution

Found in Australia and South East Asia, particularly Philippines.

Habitat

Their nests are found in forest trees.

Diet

They farm scale bugs for their honeydew, and eat small insects.

Colony size

Established colonies can reach up to half a million individuals.

Taxonomy

The weaver ants belong to the ant genus *Oecophylla* (subfamily Formicinae) which contains two closely related living species: *O. longinoda* found in Sub-Saharan Africa and *O. smaragdina* found in southern India, southeast Asia, and Australia. They are provisionally placed in a tribe of their own, Oecophyllini. The weaver ant genus *Oecophylla* is relatively old, and 15 fossil species have been found from the Eocene to Miocene deposits.

Polyrhachis and *Dendromyrmex* are two other genera of weaving ants that also use larval silk in nest construction, but the construction and architecture of their nests are simpler than those of *Oecophylla*. In Australia, *Oecophylla smaragdina* is found in the tropical coastal areas as far south as Rockhampton and across the coastal tropics of the Northern Territory down to Broome in West Australia.

The common features of the genus include an elongated first funicular segment, presence of propodeal lobes, helcium at midheight of abdominal segment 3 and gaster capable of reflexion over the mesosoma. Males have vestigial pretarsal claws.

Colony Ontogeny and Social Organization

Weaver ant colonies are founded by one or more mated females (queens). A queen lays her first clutch of eggs on a leaf and protects and feeds the larvae until they develop into mature workers. The workers then construct leaf nests and help rear new brood laid by the queen. As the number of workers increases, more nests are constructed and colony productivity and growth increase significantly. Workers perform tasks that are essential to colony survival, including foraging, nest construction, and colony defense. The exchange of information and modulation of worker behaviour that occur during worker-worker interactions are facilitated by the use of chemical and tactile communication signals.

These signals are used primarily in the contexts of foraging and colony defense. Successful foragers lay down pheromone trails that help recruit other workers to new food sources. Pheromone trails are also used by patrollers to recruit workers against territorial intruders. Along with chemical signals, workers also use tactile communication signals such as attenation and body shaking to stimulate activity in signal recipients. Multimodal communication in *Oecophylla* weaver ants importantly contribute to colony self-organization. Like many other ant species, *Oecophylla* workers exhibit social carrying behavior as part of the recruitment process, in which one worker will carry another worker in its mandibles and transport it to a location requiring attention.

Nest building behaviour

Oecophylla weaver ants are known for their remarkable cooperative behaviour used in nest construction. Possibly the first description of weaver ant's nest building behaviour was made by the English naturalist Joseph Banks, who took part in Captain James Cook's voyage to Australia in 1768. An excerpt from Joseph Banks' *Journal* (cited in Hölldobler and Wilson 1990) is included below:

The ants...one green as a leaf, and living upon trees, where it built a nest, in size between that of a man's head and his fist, by bending the leaves together, and gluing them with whitish paperish substances which held them firmly together. In doing this their management was most curious: they bend down four leaves broader than a man's hand, and place them in such a direction as they choose. This requires a much larger force than these animals seem capable of; many thousands indeed are employed in the joint work. I have seen as many as could stand by one another, holding down such a leaf, each drawing down with all his might, while others within were employed to fasten the glue. How they had bent it down I had not the opportunity of seeing, but it was held down by main strength, I easily proved by disturbing a part of them, on which the leaf bursting from the rest, returned to its natural situation, and I had an opportunity of trying with my finger the strength of these little animals must have used to get it down.

The weaver ant's ability to build capacious nests from living leaves has undeniably contributed to their ecological success. The first phase in nest construction involves workers surveying potential nesting leaves by pulling on the edges with their mandibles. When a few ants have successfully bent a leaf onto itself or drawn its edge toward another, other workers nearby join the effort. The probability of a worker joining the concerted effort is dependent on the size of the group, with workers showing a higher probability of joining when group size is large. When the span between two leaves is beyond the reach of a single ant, workers form chains with their bodies by grasping one another's petiole (waist). Multiple intricate chains working in unison are often used to ratchet together large leaves during nest construction. Once the edges of the leaves are drawn together, other workers retrieve larvae from existing nests using their mandibles. These workers hold and manipulate the larvae in such a way that causes them to excrete silk. They can only produce so much silk, so the larva will have to pupate without a cocoon. The workers then maneuver between the leaves in a highly coordinated fashion to bind them together. Weaver ant's nests are usually elliptical in shape and range in size from a single small leaf folded and bound onto itself to large nests consisting of many leaves and measure over half a meter in length. The time required to construct a nest varies depending on leaf type and eventual size, but often a large nest can be built in significantly less than 24 hours. Although weaver ant's nests are strong and impermeable to water, new nests are continually being built by workers in large colonies to replace old dying nests and those damaged by storms.

Positive and Negative Interactions with Crop Plants

Large colonies of *Oecophylla* weaver ants consume significant amounts of food, and workers continuously kill a variety of arthropods (primarily insects) close to their nests. Insects are not only consumed by workers, but this protein source is necessary for brood development. Because weaver ant workers hunt and kill insects that are potentially harmful plant pests, trees harboring weaver ants benefit from having decreased levels of herbivory. They have traditionally been used in biological control in Chinese and Southeast Asian citrus orchards from at least 400 AD. Many studies have shown the efficacy of using weaver ants as natural biocontrol agents against agricultural pests. The use of weaver ants as biocontrol agents has especially been effective for fruit agriculture, particularly in Australia and southeast Asia. Fruit trees harboring weaver ants produce higher quality fruits, show less leaf damage by herbivores, and require fewer applications of synthetic pesticides. Farmers in southeast Asia often build rope bridges between trees and orchards to actively recruit ants to unoccupied trees. Established colonies are often supplemented with food to promote faster growth and to deter emigration.

Oecophylla colonies may not be entirely beneficial to the host plants. Studies indicate that the presence of *Oecophylla* colonies may also have negative effects on the performance of host plants by reducing fruit removal by mammals and birds and therefore reducing seed dispersal and by lowering the flower-visiting rate of flying insects including pollinators. Weaver ants also have an adverse effect on tree productivity by protecting sap feeding insects such as scale insects and leafhoppers from which they collect honeydew. By protecting these insects from predators they increase their population and increase the damage they cause to trees.

Role in the Habitat

Weaver Ants are exploited by plants and animals. Some plants such as the Sea Hibiscus (*Hibiscus tiliceaus*) secrete nectar in their leaves to attract these ants, which in turn protect the plant from insect leaf eaters. The nasty bite of the ants also discourages larger herbivores. Another plant that does the same is the Great Morinda (*Morinda citrifolia*). Weaver Ants' nests are often found in these two plants at Sungei Buloh Nature Park.

Some other creatures also exploit the Weaver Ant's sweet tooth. Some caterpillars of the Lycaenidae and Noctuidae butterfly families secrete a honey dew that attracts these ants to protect them. Some of these caterpillars are more sinister and use their bribe to gain entry into the ant's nest and devour their larvae! Some jumping spiders look and more importantly, smell like ants, and in their disguise, enter the ant's nest to devour them and their larvae.

Status and Threats

Weaver Ant eggs (i.e., pupae) are harvested and sold in markets in Thailand and the Philippines. The taste of the pupae has been described as creamy. The adults are also eaten, their taste has been described as lemony or creamy and sour. The Dayaks in Borneo mix adult ants with their rice for flavouring. Needless to say, harvesting these fiercely biting ants requires good technique!

THE USES OF WEAVER ANTS

Ant Eaters

Weaver ant pupae are harvested and sold as food in markets in Thailand and the Philippines.The taste of the pupae has been described as creamy flavor. People also eat adult weaver ants. Their taste is described as lemony or creamy and sour. The Dayaks in Borneo mix adult ants with rice for extra texture and flavor. Weaver ants are fierce biters, so people who harvest them have to be extra careful!

Use as Traditional Medicines

People who live near weaver ants sometimes use them as a type of medicine. The ants have a strong chemical in their bodies called formic acid. The ants use the formic acid to protect their nests. People have discovered that they can collect a few of the worker ants and crush them to make a special mixture. The mixture is then used to fight infections. This kind of medicine is called traditional medicine. Studying traditional medicines like this may help scientists find new methods to cure diseases.

The larvae and pupae are collected and processed into bird food, fish bait and in the production of traditional medicines in Thailand , Vietnam and Indonesia.

Use as a Living Insecticide

The ancient Chinese as early as in AD 300, exploited the voracious appetite of these ants by using them to control insect pests in their citrus orchards. They use them to control insect pests in their citrus orchards. To do this, they first put a weaver ant nest in an orchard. Then, they place bamboo strips among the trees to serve as "ant bridges." These ant bridges encourage the ants to colonize all the trees. More fruit growers are now bringing back this traditional practice of using weaver ants for pest control. It is a cheaper way of dealing with insects that have developed resistance to chemical insecticides.

Large colonies of *Oecophylla* weaver ants consume significant amounts of food, and workers continuously kill a variety of arthropods (primarily insects) close to their nests. Insects are not only consumed by workers, but this protein source is necessary for brood development.

Because weaver ant workers hunt and kill insects that are potentially harmful plant pests, trees harboring weaver ants benefit from having decreased levels of herbivory. They have traditionally been used in biological control in Chinese and Southeast Asian citrus orchards from at least 400 AD. Many studies have shown the efficacy of using weaver ants as natural biocontrol agents against agricultural pests.

The use of weaver ants as biocontrol agents has especially been effective for fruit agriculture, particularly in Australia and southeast Asia. Fruit trees harboring weaver ants produce higher quality fruits, show less leaf damage by herbivores, and require fewer applications of synthetic pesticides.

Farmers in Southeast Asia often build rope bridges between trees and orchards to actively recruit ants to unoccupied trees. Established colonies are often supplemented with food to promote faster growth and to deter emigration.

Today in plant production, Weaver ants are usud in biocontrol to kill many kinds of insects on plant fruit trees. Their type: generalist predator and their hosts: citrus stinkbug, leaf-feeding caterpillars, aphids, citrus leafminer, leafhoppers, plant hoppers, bugs, moths, adult black bugs, and small animals.

In Mekong delta of Vietnam, weaver ants are used as living pesticides to kill many insect species on fruit plant trees from hundreds of years to now a day.

Conservation and Management

Weaver ants thrive well in undisturbed places and plenty of green leaves. Plant fruit trees or shrubs in or around your new citrus orchard however, banana, sapodilla, and papaya are less suitable.

Introduce only native weaver ants to the orchard when no black ants' species are present to ensure the establishment of a weaver ant colony.

Provide them with food during the dry season such as dried fish and shrimp, cut into pieces that are small enough for the individual ant to carry.

Put bamboo or wooden strips between trees to guide the ants to transfer from one tree to another for them to build new colonies in other trees.

To expand weaver ants' colonies to other field crops, tie a rope to a tree where they live, to guide them to the areas you want them to colonize. Monitor regularly the ant colonies. Like other insects, ants are easily being killed by pesticide.

16

The Importance of Weaver Ant (*Oecophylla smaragdina* Fabricius)

INTRODUCTION

The weaver ants belonging to the genus *Oecophylla* consist of two extant species - *O. smaragdina* which is distributed throughout tropical Asia, Australasia and some Pacific islands and *O. longinoda* distributed throughout tropical Africa. The species share similar biological and ecological characteristics. They are both polydomous canopy ants that build leaf nests on their host trees. Nests are constructed by drawing together leaves and fixing them with silk produced from their larvae. The nests are easily visible and scattered throughout the canopy territory of the ants which can cover up to 1500 m2 for a single large colony. The ants use a wide range of host trees and prefer sunny habitats.

Therefore they are usually abundant in disturbed habitats with trees or bushes. Weaver ants are aggressive and will prey on most arthropods entering their territory and additionally scavenge on a wide range of organisms including vertebrates. Due to their predatory habit *Oecophylla* ants are recognised as biological control agents in tropical tree crops as they are able to protect a variety of crops against many different insect pests. In this way they are utilised indirectly as an alternative to chemical insecticides. It is less well known that the ants can be utilised directly also, as a commercial product. There exist at least three different markets for the use of these ants in Southeast Asia:

(i) in Chinese and Indian traditional medicines,

(ii) as a valued feed for song birds in Indonesia, and

(iii) as a prized human delicacy in Thailand and other Asian countries.

In Chhattisgarh, India, traditional healers believe that regular intake of *O. smaragdina* will prevent rheumatism – a view shared by practitioners of traditional Chinese medicine. The Indian healers also prepare oils in which they dip collected ants. After 40 days oils are used externally to cure rheumatism, gout, ringworm or other skin diseases, or else as an aphrodisiac.

In Java there is great enthusiasm for keeping captive songbirds. According to bird lovers the larvae and pupae of *O. smaragdina* provide essential protein and vitamins to their birds and so will improve the bird's performance. For use as a bird food they are willing to pay up to US$1.4 per kg of ant brood. Lower-quality ant brood is used to feed chickens where it is believed to accelerate feather growth and flesh production. The tradition of including *Oecophylla* ants in food and/or traditional medicine has been reported from various cultures in Thailand, India, Myanmar, Borneo, Philippines, Papua New Guinea, Australia and Congo. Especially in Thailand *O. smaragdina* is considered a delicacy and has been eaten by humans for centuries. Imagos as well as brood are used in a variety of Thai dishes and are easily obtained on many local markets throughout the country during the ant harvest season. Larvae and pupae are preferred over imagos and the queen caste preferred over the worker castes and males. The season in which *O. smaragdina* produce new queens therefore defines the ant harvest season.

The ants are used as ingredients in soups, salads and fried dishes and sometimes eaten raw together with spices as a snack. The tradition of eating ants is most prominent among the Isaan people of Northeast Thailand and the people in Northern Thailand but has spread to other parts of the country with the migration of people from these cultures. A growing interest in the eating of ants has led to higher demand throughout Thailand with increasing prices as a result. Thus, the collection of ants is becoming more profitable and the harvest pressure on local *O. smaragdina* populations may increase accordingly, potentially leading to an unsustainable overexploitation of these ants in natural habitats.

The purpose of the present paper is to assess the socio-economic significance of ant harvesting and thereby evaluate the potential future pressure on this resource. We seek to identify factors that limit the trade, and conduct a preliminary assessment of the need for alternatives to the harvest of naturally occurring populations in order to prevent future over-harvesting of ants. In this context we discuss the development of ant farming as a way to prevent the unsustainable utilisation of ants as a food resource. Thailand is one of the countries where the utilisation of ants as a natural food resource is most prominent and organised, with the harvest of *O. smaragdina* in Northeastern Thailand particularly developed. The harvest of this ant in a province in Northeastern Thailand was therefore selected for the study.

Methodology

In 2005 a survey was conducted to document and elucidate the extent of *O. smaragdina* harvesting in Northeastern Thailand and its contribution to local livelihoods. Seven villages located in two districts, around Kasetsart University´s Forestry Student Training Station in Nakhon Ratchasima Province, were chosen at random. In the year 2000 Nakhon Ratchasima Province had a population of 2,565,685 people with a median age of 29 years and a sex ratio of 97 (males per hundred females). Sixty-six percent of the population worked within the agricultural sector and 31% of the population was self-employed, 33% was employees and 36% were unpaid family workers. The two districts covered an area of 2,504 km^2 with a total of 296 villages and a population of 156,576 people, of whom 64% were between 15 and 59 years old. While population data for the individual study villages was unavailable, average village size was therefore 534 persons (ignoring the fraction of the population living in cities). The national forest area in the vicinity of the villages was mainly composed of dry deciduous dipterocarp forest, which is characterised by a limited soil layer on a rocky surface. The result is a landscape with low tree density, an open canopy and sparse and dry undergrowth affected by regular fires. Due to the open canopy and limited tree height it is easy to detect and harvest *O. smaragdina* nests in this habitat. In the seven villages all people collecting *O. smaragdina* were interviewed using structured questionnaires. The questions were centred on methods used to collect ants, yields, location of activities (spatially and temporally), challenges associated with the profession and the economy associated with ant harvesting. The questionnaire survey was conducted by Wissanurak Sribandit between 1 March and 30 April 2006 and all questions referred to ant harvesting activities carried out by ant collectors during 2004 and 2005.

Secondly, more than ten ant harvesters were observed in the field in April 2006, February 2007 and April 2007 in order to describe the methods used to harvest the ants. Variation measures (±) given in the results refer to standard deviation. The currency exchange rate used between THB and US$ was 1:0.02936.

Results

In the seven villages a total of 25 people between 41 and 62 years were harvesting ants (mean = 3.57 ± 4.12 persons village-1). Given an estimated 349 in each village within the age group 15 to 59 years (an overestimate as some of these worked in cities), at least 1% of the working population was harvesting ants. Four collectors were men, 21 were women and the average size of their households was 4.6 (±1.89) persons. All 25 persons were interviewed for the study. Ants were harvested mainly in national forests, where 76% of the harvesters collected ants, and secondly in villages and farm areas, where 40% collected ants. Only 8% harvested ants in plantation areas (percentages exceed 100 since some people harvest in more than one type of habitat). Assuming the seven villages' ant 'catchment area' was an equal share of the two districts, the 25 collectors used an area of approximately 59 km^2.

Ant Harvesting Techniques

All collectors used the same method to harvest ants: ants were harvested from the early morning when the ants were least active and until midday. A long (6-10 m) bamboo stick with a net mounted close to the pointed tip was used to pierce the *Oecophylla* leaf nests. When the bamboo stick was shaken, imago worker ants (hereafter called workers), imago virgin queens (hereafter called virgin queens) and brood dropped into the net (Figs. 16.1-16.3).

From the net the ants were poured into a bucket with water enabling the collectors to separate the different ant castes and developmental stages. Workers were separated from virgin queens and imagos were separated from the brood which comprised both larvae and pupae (Figs. 15.6-16.5).

After separation the ants were either kept in a refrigerator or stored in water at ambient temperature. In this way it was claimed that ant brood could stay fresh for up to 12 days. As a protection against ant bites, collectors used rubber boots powdered with fine starch powder. The combination of rubber and fine powder prevented the ants from crossing the boots.

The same powder was also used on hands and on the bamboo stick to impede ant attacks. The ant harvest started in January when 16% of the collectors were active, peaked in February-April when 80-92% were active, and ceased in May during which only 8% were collecting ants. Outside this season none of the collectors harvested ants.

Fig. 16.1. A Thai ant collector harvesting an Oecophylla nest on a mango tree.

Fig. 16.2. Harvesting net filled with freshly collected ants.

Fig. 16.3: An ant collector separating workers from brood by dusting the ants with starch powder on a tray. Worker ants seem to be repelled by the powder, and try to flee without the brood.

Fig. 16.4. Ant collectors processing the harvest: separating workers from virgin queens and imagos from brood (larvae and pupae).

Fig. 16.5. The final fresh product of queen larvae and pupae ready for the market.

Harvest Yields

When collectors were asked to estimate their daily yields they reported that the harvest per working day averaged 2.88 (± 1.78) kg brood, 1.58 (± 1.45) kg virgin queens and 0.08 (± 0.39) kg workers (only one person reported harvesting workers, at 2.0 kg workers day^{-1}), resulting in a daily total of 4.54 (± 2.24) kg ants collector^{-1}. When asked to estimate their harvest yields by month and summing these numbers, it emerged that brood yield peaked in February-March whereas virgin-queen yield peaked in April.

In total the collectors harvested an estimated 5486 kg ants year-1; thus each person collected on average 219.4 (± 107.5) kg ants year^{-1} (or season^{-1}). Each collected ants on an average of 48 days [(5486 kg/4.54 kg/day)/25 ant collectors)] during the season. Assuming 254 working days in a year the average time spent by collectors on ant collection thus equalled 19% of the working year. However, the collectors did not spend the whole day but on average only 4.48 (± 1.73) hours working-day-1 on the collection of ants (ignoring the time spent selling the ants in the market, which was not recorded in this study) resulting in 10-11% of the working year.

Trading and Selling Prices

Nine collectors sold all their harvest at markets, four used the entire harvest for the family, one sold all in the village and one sold all to middlemen. The remaining ten collectors sold their harvest to more than one purchaser. On average ant collectors estimated that 50.6 (± 18.2)% (219 kg year^{-1} × 0.506 = 111 kg year^{-1}) of the harvest was sold at town markets, 22.4 (± 41.1)% (= 49 kg year^{-1}) was eaten by the family, 13.2 (± 33.4)% (= 29 kg year^{-1}) was sold in the village, 10.2 (± 39.0)% (= 22 kg year^{-1}) was sold to middlemen and 3.6 (± 0.0)% (= 8 kg year^{-1}) was sold to restaurants. The market price of brood and virgin queens ranged from 100-200

THB (US$2.94-5.87) kg^{-1} with higher minimum prices at both ends of the season; in January and May minimum prices were between 120 and 180 THB (US$3.52-5.28) kg^{-1} depending on the year. The interview data lack information on the price of workers, but we observed workers being sold for 50 THB (US$1.47) kg^{-1} at the market in Pak Tong Chai. In general the highest prices were obtained at the town markets (~200 THB) whereas middlemen, restaurants and people from the villages paid less. In one case a collector obtained

Costs and Income

Among the ant collectors the lowest reported total cost associated with ant harvesting was 30 THB (US$0.88) working-day^{-1} whereas the highest was 550 THB (US$16.15) working-day^{-1}, with time (52%, calculated based on the minimum daily wage and the fraction of the day spent collecting) and travel costs (47%) making up 99% of the total and equipment making up only 1%. Travel costs to ant sites were more costly (29%)

than travel to markets (18%); collectors travelled between 0.1 and 80 km to ant sites with an average of 16.5 (± 21.69) km working-day^{-1}.

Among the ant collectors the total gross yearly income of the household ranged between a minimum of 18,000 THB (US$528) and a maximum of 115,000 THB (US$3376) (mean = 67,154 ± 27,652 THB, = US$1971 ± 812), whereas the yearly gross income from ant harvesting ranged from 4,000 (US$117.4) to 50,000 THB (US$1468) (mean = 19,884 ± 13,317 THB, = US$584 ± 391) (Table 16.1).

For individual collectors the yearly income from ant harvesting thus constituted between 10% and 69% of the total yearly income with a mean of 30% (Table 16.1). Based on the yearly income and average number of working days the daily gross and net incomes from the ant harvest equalled 411 THB (US$12.07) and 236 THB (US$6.93) working-day^{-1}, respectively. In Nakhon Ratchasima Province the legal minimum wage (and the wage often paid to manual workers) equals 162 THB (US$4.76) day^{-1} (8 hr). Thus the net income from ant harvests was approximately 1.5 times the minimum wage for the province, or 2.6 times if it is considered that only 4.48 hours working day^{-1} were spent on ant collection.

Constraints

Eighty-four percent of the collectors reported finding it increasingly difficult to harvest ants compared to earlier years. Among these 76% considered an increasing number of ant collectors problematic, whereas 24% found increasing travel distance a problem and 8% had problems with obtaining permits. On the other hand, all collectors found it easy to sell their harvest. Forty-eight percent of the interviewed collectors were interested in establishing commercial ant farms to make collection easier and more profitable (52% showed no interest) but only 12% had ideas about how to develop ant farming.

Discussion

Economic Importance

On average more than three people per village (at least 1% of the working population) collected ants, each collecting almost 220 kg of ant brood during the 4-5-month ant harvesting season. The ant-harvesting income constituted on average 30% (Table 16.1) of the collectors' yearly household income, yet collecting ants took up only between 10 and 19% of a working year; thus the earnings from the ant harvest exceeded those of other activities for an average collector. Daily net income from ant harvesting was 1.5-2.6 times higher than the minimum daily salary for the area. If these figures are typical for villages of the province, wild *Oecophylla* collection is currently worth some 21 million THB (US$620,000) per year in Nakhon Ratchasima. Furthermore, not only collectors were supported by the ant trade. Despite the high price of ant brood (200 THB kg^{-1} at markets compared with chicken, pork and beef with price ranges of 60-70, 90-100 and 100-120 THB kg^{-1}, respectively) ants were easy to sell and trading via middlemen and restaurants generated incomes to these other links in the trading network.

Additionally, the harvest constituted a substantial part of the family food intake with an average consumption of 49 kg of ants per season in each collector family. We therefore conclude that the harvest of *Oecophylla* ants in the Nakhon Ratchasima area supports a substantial part of the local community, yielding above-average cash income and important nutrients. The importance of the ant trade to local labour is further pronounced by the timing of the season which is at the end of the dry season when the need for farming labour is minimal and thus alternative incomes are low.

Sustainability

The 25 collectors harvested more than 5 tonnes of ants per season from a roughly-estimated catchment area of 59 km2; this translates to 93 kg km^{-2} $season^{-1}$.

Table 16.2. The estimated total yearly household incomes and incomes from the ant harvest for individual ant collectors, in Thai Baht (THB). Empty entries show collectors that were unable to estimate their yearly income from ant harvest. F = female, M = male.

Ant collector	Gender	Total income (THB)	Income from ant harvest (THB)	Ant income / total income
1	F	18,000	-	-
2	F	24,500	5,000	0.20
3	F	25,000	4,000	0.16
4	F	38,500	4,900	0.13
5	M	40,200	5,500	0.14
6	F	46,100	-	-
7	F	52,000	5,100	0.10
8	F	71,000	12,000	0.17
9	F	75,500	13,500	0.18
10	M	67,000	16,500	0.25
11	F	75,000	12,500	0.17
12	F	79,000	13,500	0.17
13	F	80,000	-	-
14	F	69,000	15,500	0.22
15	F	55,000	30,500	0.55
16	F	60,000	31,500	0.53
17	F	45,050	31,000	0.69
18	F	50,000	-	-
19	F	85,000	32,500	0.38
20	F	115,000	30,300	0.26
21	M	95,000	32,000	0.34
22	M	105,000	50,000	0.48
23	F	98,000	-	-
24	F	110,000	-	-
25	F	100,000	32,000	0.32
N	25	19	19	
Average	67,154	19,884	0.30	
SD	27,652	13,317	0.17	

Harvesters reported they had no impression of a decline in the number of ant colonies in the area. This observation suggests that the harvest at present is sustainable. One reason is the Thai preference for the large virgin queen ants. They only harvest during the queen production season and only collect from the largest nest where the queen brood is located.

Smaller nests, where the founding queen and worker brood is located, are not harvested from the colonies. The worker ant population is therefore only marginally reduced and the founding queen rarely damaged. Thus, the colony survival are maintained. In contrast, the newly produced queens (and males) are not essential to colony survival since they eventually leave the colony for mating and establishment of new colonies; the newly mated queens can be collected individually or in small clusters in the vegetation during the mating season.

This is also supported by our observations that the harvest of ants in an experimental mango plantation in the same area did not affect worker ant densities negatively; all harvested colonies were still present after one year and worker ant densities were actually higher in harvested compared to unharvested colonies.

On the other hand, the number of ant collectors was increasing. Inexperienced newcomers may, in order to increase yield, adopt harvesting techniques (for example harvesting small nests) that do not consider sustainability. We do not have information on how long ant collection has been practised in the area, but it is believed to be for many generations, and certain traditional practices have been beneficial to sustainability.

For example the normal size of the holes in the collecting net enables the majority of workers and worker brood to escape. However, some collectors used densely woven material with the result that all the contents of the nests would be collected. Also, new ant collectors may be unaware of the ant's biology. They could harvest more than one ant territory at a time with the result that workers from different colonies become mixed and start fighting inside ant territories. This may again reduce worker densities and leave the colonies with weakened defences, as well as introducing hostile non nest-mate workers in proximity to the founding queens and thereby putting them at risk.

A high economic incentive to harvest ants as documented in this study will probably result in a steadily increase of ant collectors and increasing competition. Thus, higher harvest pressures and temptations to adopt unsustainable harvesting methods may result. It is therefore likely that the natural ant population may be put at risk in the future as it has been seen in Java where *Oecophylla* ants have become scarce in some areas due to high harvest pressures. The increasing numbers of ant collectors, long travel distances and associated costs have made accessibility to ant sites an important economic parameter.

Ant Farming

Ant farming may become a possible solution, to both future over-harvesting of natural populations and increasing costs associated with travelling to ant sites. By limited intervention it is possible to establish or increase ant yield in nearby crop and non-crop trees. If trees are not sprayed with insecticides *Oecophylla* colonies may establish naturally (they occur on most mango and pomelo trees in the vicinity) or, alternatively, they may be artificially introduced. Subsequent separation of neighbouring colonies to prevent fighting and the provision of food and water may then increase the yield of harvestable queen brood and generate a profit. Even in fruit plantations ant farming may be profitable since *Oecophylla* spp. can protect a variety of crop trees against pest insects and because the harvest does not markedly reduce the densities of worker ants (the caste that patrol the trees for pests).

It follows that biocontrol by *O. smaragdina* may be retained under ant harvesting regimes. The establishment of ant farming may reduce costs not only by creating high-density ant sites closer to villages but also by making the harvest of ants less time-consuming, since cultured trees are usually smaller and thus more easily accessible than trees in natural forests, where the majority of the harvest (76%) is collected at present. The active farming of ants may thus reduce the pressure on natural populations. This view is supported by the 48% of collectors who showed interest in ant farming. Development of ant farming thus offers an option to maintain economic and ecological sustainability in ant harvesting.

Parallels between Thai and Indonesian *Oecophylla* Harvesting

To our knowledge only one other study has described traditional *Oecophylla* harvesting in detail. As outlined in the introduction scientist describes the harvest of *Oecophylla* brood in Indonesia where ants are used as bird food. According to researcherthe Indonesian harvesting technique was almost identical to the Thai technique using long bamboo poles with a net to harvest the ant nests. In Indonesia, though, collectors reported that the high-quality brood (worker brood) could only be stored for approximately two days whereas the Thais claimed to be able to store brood for up to 12 days. This difference may arise because the Thais refer to the storing of virgin queen brood whereas Indonesian collectors refer to the storage of worker brood.

Actually, the Indonesians mention that larger larvae can be stored for longer. In both countries the production of sexual brood seems to take place during the dry season, but Indonesian collectors regard the wet season with worker brood as the high-quality season whereas the Thais in this study only harvest ants during the dry season, when virgin queens are produced. Daily yields from the dry season are similar between the countries with an average of 2-5 kg per person per day in Indonesia in comparison to the 4.5 kg reported from the present study. In the wet season when the ant larvae are smaller the daily Indonesian average was 1.5 kg.

A striking difference between the two markets was in the market price of ant brood. The consumer price was similar in the two countries, at approximately US$5 kg^{-1} (if the THBUS$

conversion rate is corrected to the 2004 rate = 0.025). However, Indonesian collectors obtained only US$1.2-1.4 kg^{-1} when they sold their harvest to middlemen. In contrast Thai collectors only used middlemen for a minor part (14%) of the harvest and the price difference between middlemen and local markets was small (11% difference in one case).

The high price difference in Indonesia is probably based on the long distance between ant sites and consumer markets which are mainly situated in larger cities. Therefore middlemen with high transportation costs are needed in the Indonesian trade chain. Both Indonesian and Thai collectors could easily sell all their harvest quickly indicating high demand in both countries.

Consumers in Indonesia were reported to have to wait for their produce to arrive. Due to high demand Indonesian collectors also reported increasing competition for the resource and newcomers to the profession as well as old collectors often disregarded the former harvesting techniques developed to ensure sustainability. For example, harvesting rotation intervals were being violated with the result that *Oecophylla* was becoming scarce in several exploited areas on Java.

Implication for Biocontrol

Often the biting of *Oecophylla* ants is a major complaint envisaged by plantation managers when advised to use the ants for biological control and this may hinder implementation of this environment-friendly technology. It is worth noting that the Thai ant collectors described in this study have been able to develop techniques to avoid unacceptable levels of ant bites, even though they are disturbing the ant nests which are the most fiercely protected part of the ant territory. The ant collection methods developed by the Thais may be utilised to avoid ant bites among plantation workers in *Oecophylla* protected crops and facilitate the implementation of *Oecophylla* biocontrol.

Future Directions

In conclusion, the harvest of *Oecophylla* ants in Northeast Thailand is substantial and not only for local subsistence but an effective way of earning cash. There is an economically-driven, increasing interest in harvesting ants and thus increasing pressure on natural ant populations. Ant farming may be a solution to retain sustainability and at the same time enhance profitability. Further studies are needed to develop ant farming and test the profitability of different management practises.

They include identifying the ants' food requirements (carbohydrates vs. protein) and the food conversion efficiencies of different kinds of food, locating easily-accessible, cheap and sustainable protein sources, and investigating impacts on existing biotic communities, including populations of other economically beneficial invertebrates. Also, studies examining the effect of ant harvest pressures on local ant populations are needed to verify the sustainability of the present activities.

17

Worker Ant Community in the Gilimale Forest Reserve

Introduction

Since 1955, Gilimale Forest Reserve in Sri Lanka has been known as a habitat of the Sri Lanka-endemic ant, *Aneuretus simoni* Emery (Wilson *et al*. 1956; Jayasuriya & Traniello 1985), the sole extant representative of Subfamily Aneuretinae. Gilimale Forest Reserve (6° 472 N and 80° 282 E, average altitude 152 m) occupies approximately 1,147 ha and is situated in Ratnapura District, in Sabaragamuwa Province. This wet evergreen tropical forest receives on average 4,758 mm of rainfall annually and is characterised by highly dissected terrain with numerous streams draining into several rivers. The average slope ranges from 9o to 15o, but certain areas adjoining streams and rivers are extremely steep.

Eleven ant genera (*Aneuretus, Camponotus, Crematogaster, Euponera* (*Brachyponera*), *Euponera* (*Mesoponera*), *Myrmicaria, Paratrechina* (*Nylanderia*), *Pheidole, Ponera, Polyrhachis* and *Technomyrmex*) were recorded from the forest, whereas ten genera (*Aneuretus, Camponotus, Crematogaster, Monomorium, Odontomachus, Pachycondyla, Paratrechina, Ponera, Solenopsis* and *Tetramorium*) were recorded by researchers. Our first survey of Gilimale Forest, in February 2004, revealed nine subfamilies (Aenictinae, Amblyoponinae, Aneuretinae, Dolichoderinae,

Dorylinae, Formicinae, Leptanillinae, Myrmicinae and Ponerinae) and 37 species including *A. simoni*. The survey was extended through October and December 2004 and the results of the six visits are combined here to characterise the community of ground-dwelling ants observed by simultaneous multiple sampling in Gilimale Forest throughout 2004. We also report on several ecological aspects of *A. simoni* workers in this forest.

Field and Laboratory Methods

Ten locations of Gilimale Forest Reserve were surveyed for ants, using several sampling methods along a 100 m transect laid at each location, on 23–26 February, 15–18 April, 24–27 June, 24–27 August, 29–31 October and 17–19 December 2004. At each location we carried out extraction of ants by (a) mini-Winkler sacks, (b) soil sifting, (c) pitfall trapping, (d & e) honey and canned fish baiting, (f) litter sifting by hand and (g) timed hand collection. Within each transect:

(a) Five polythene bags were each filled with leaf litter from five different 1 m2 areas, sampled at 20 m intervals along the transect, and the litter in each bag was transferred to a mini-Winkler sack kept in the laboratory. The worker ants emerging after 48 hours were preserved in 85% ethanol.

(b) Ten soil samples (each 20 × 20 wide × 10 cm deep), taken at 10 m intervals along a line which was parallel and one m left of the transect, were sifted through mesh into a white tray. All ants seen with the naked eye were collected into glass vials filled with 85% ethanol.

(c) Ten cups (volume: 110 cm^3), each half-filled with soap water, were set in the soil at 10 m intervals along a line parallel and 1 m right of the transect, with the mouth of the cups flush with the surface soil level.

(d, e) Twenty-five baits each of honey and canned fish (jack mackerel in natural juice with added salt), on a 5 × 5 cm piece of gauze, were placed alternately on the ground at 4 m intervals along the transect, and the pieces of gauze and attending ants were collected after one hour into a plastic bottle filled with 50% ethanol.

(f) Ten litter samples (each of one full sieve), taken at 10 m intervals along the transects, were sifted into a white tray and ants seen with the naked eye were collected into a vial filled with 85% ethanol.

(g) Hand collection was conducted for 10 minutes, around a point approximately 10 m apart from the next, with ten such points in each transect. At each point, ants crawling on the forest floor along a horizontal line which connects each point at 1 m left and 1 m right of the transect, were collected and ants were preserved in 85% ethanol.

Some of the locations were also sampled at night by different methods: (h) honey-baited pitfall traps on the ground and (i) honey-baited small plastic vials hung on trees.

(h) In three of the transects used during the daytime, ten plastic cups of 110 cm3, each honey-baited and half-filled with 50% ethanol, were set in the evening in the soil along the 100 m transect.

(i) At the same three locations in February, and five locations on subsequent occasions, ten honey-baited small plastic vials were hung in the evenings (17:00–18:00 h) on ten trees, 10 m apart along the transects, and were collected at around 07:00 h the following morning.

Collected ants were preserved in 85% ethanol and the presence of *A. simoni* and other species was recorded. Ants were identified to the furthest possible taxonomic level using a low-power stereo-microscope at suitable magnifications.

Measurement of environmental parameters during the sampling of ants

During each survey, air and soil temperature at the start, middle and end points of each transect were measured using a thermometer and the mean value per transect was recorded. Depth of the leaf litter layer was measured in the same manner using a ruler, and the mean depth (cm) per transect was recorded. Similarly, three subsamples of soil from each transect were brought to the laboratory and soil humidity of each transect was recorded. The mean value of each parameter during the sampling period was calculated from the ten locations measured on each occasion.

Results

Species Richness and Composition of Worker Ant Community

Table 17.1 shows that worker ants belonging to 11 subfamilies, 38 genera and 50 species were recorded from the six visits to Gilimale Forest in 2004. The number of subfamilies observed on each occasion was 9, 8, 6, 9, 7 and 6, respectively. Seventeen species [*Aneuretus simoni* Emery, *Camponotus* sp. 1, *Carebara* sp., *Dolichoderus* sp. 1, *Lophomyrmex quadrispinosus* (Jerdon), *Leptogenys* sp., *Monomorium* sp., *Myrmicaria brunnea* Saunders, *Odontomachus simillimus* F. Smith, *Paratrechina* (sensu lato) sp., *Pheidole* sp. 2, *Pheidole* sp. 7, *Pheidologeton diversus* (Jerdon), *Polyrhachis* sp., *Solenopsis* sp., *Technomyrmex bicolor* Emery and *Tetramorium bicarinatum* (Nylander)] were common on all occasions and observed throughout the study period. In addition, *Acropyga acutiventris* Roger, *Cardiocondyla* sp., *Cerapachys* sp., *Dorylus* sp., *Pachycondyla* sp. 3, *Pheidole* sp. 8 and *Tetraponera allaborans* (Walker) were observed on two or more of the six visits. The highest species richness was recorded in February, whereas lowest species richness was observed in December.

Table 17.1: Worker ant species observed on each visit to Gilimale Forest and overall worker ant community recorded in 2004. Bold letters show the species observed on all occasions. p = present

Subfamily	Genus/ species	Visit						Overall
		1	2	3	4	5	6	
1. Aenictinae	1) *Aenictus* sp.	p	p	-	p	-	-	P
2. Amblyoponinae	2) *Amblyopone* sp.	p	p	-	p	-	p	P
3. Aneuretinae	3) *Aneuretus simoni*	p	p	p	p	p	p	P
4. Cerapachyinae	4) *Cerapachys* sp.	-	p	-	-	-	-	P
5. Dorylinae	5) *Dorylus* sp.	p	-	-	-	-	-	P
6. Dolichoderinae	**6) *Dolichoderus* sp. 1**	**p**	**p**	**p**	**p**	**p**	**p**	**P**
	7) *Tapinoma indicum*	p	-	-	p	-	-	P
	8) *T. melanocephalum*	-	-	p	p	p	-	P
	9) *Technomyrmex bicolor*	p	p	p	p	p	p	P
	10) *T. albipes*	p	-	p	p	p	p	P
7. Formicinae	11) *Acropyga acutiventris*	-	-	-	-	-	p	P
	12) *Anoplolepis gracilipes*	p	p	p	p	-	-	P
	13) *Camponotus* sp. 1	p	p	p	p	p	p	P
	14) C. sp. 2	p	p	p	p	-	-	P

	15)	*Lepisiota* sp.	p	-	-	-	-	-	P
	16)	*Myrmoteras* sp.	p	-	p	-	-	p	P
	17)	*Paratrechina** sp.	p	p	p	p	p	p	P
	18)	*P. longicornis*	p	-	-	p	p	-	P
	19)	*Polyrhachis* sp.	p	p	p	p	p	p	P
	20)	*Pseudolasius* sp.	-	-	p	p	p	-	P
8. Leptanillinae	21)	*Leptanilla* sp.	p	-	p	p	p	-	P
9. Myrmicinae	22)	*Calyptomyrmex* sp.	-	-	p	p	p	-	P
	23)	*Cardiocondyla* sp.	p	-	-	-	-	-	P
	24)	*Carebara* sp.	p	p	p	p	p	p	P
	25)	*Cataulacus* sp.	-	p	p	p	-	-	P
	26)	*Crematogaster* sp. 1	p	p	p	p	p	-	P
	27)	*C.* sp. 2	p	-	-	-	-	p	P
	28)	*C.* sp. 3	p	-	-	-	-	p	P
	29)	*Lophomyrmex quadrispinosus*	p	p	p	p	p	p	P
	30)	*Meranoplus bicolor*	-	-	p	p	p	-	P
	31)	*Monomorium* sp.	p	p	p	p	p	p	P
	32)	*Myrmicaria brunnea*	p	p	p	p	p	p	P
	33)	*Pheidole* sp. 2	p	p	p	p	p	p	P
	34)	*P.* sp. 7	p	p	p	p	p	p	P

Subfamily		Genus/ species	Visit						Overall
			1	2	3	4	5	6	
	35)	*P.* sp. 8	p	-	-	-	-	p	P
	36)	*Pheidologeton* sp.	p	p	p	p	P	p	P
	37)	*Solenopsis* sp.	p	p	p	p	P	p	P
	38)	*Strumigenys (Quadristruma)* sp.	p	p	p	p	P	-	P
	39)	*Tetramorium* sp.	p	p	p	-	P	p	P
	40)	*T. bicarinatum*	p	p	p	p	P	p	P
10. Ponerinae	41)	*Anochetus* sp.	p	p	-	p	P	p	P
	42)	*Centromyrmex feae*	p	p	p	-	P	-	P
	43)	*Hypoponera* sp.	p	p	p	p	P	-	p
	44)	*Leptogenys* sp.	p	p	p	p	P	p	p
	45)	*Odontomachus simillimus*	p	p	p	p	P	p	p
	46)	*Ponera* sp.	p	p	p	p	-	p	p
	47)	*Pachycondyla* sp. 1	-	p	p	-	P	p	p
	48)	*P.* sp. 2	-	p	-	-	P	-	p
	49)	*P.* sp. 3	-	-	-	-	-	p	p
11. Pseudomyrmecinae	50)	*Tetraponera allaborans*	-	-	-	p	P	-	p
Total			39	32	34	36	33	29	50

Effects of using several sampling methods and transects on recorded species richness

Employing a combination of several simultaneous sampling methods yielded more ant species than using a single method on each occasion (Table 17.2). The cumulative number of species observed during this study increased with the number of transects (to ten) and visits (to six).

Table 17.2: Species richness recorded by each sampling method and the overall methods on each visit to Gilimale Forest. Only daytime sampling methods used at all sites are shown

Month	CB	HB	LS	SS	HC	CB+HB+LS +SS+HC
February	19	24	27	22	17	39
April	17	19	22	14	24	32
June	20	19	20	15	20	32
August	22	21	23	12	16	36
October	16	21	17	13	22	32
December	11	13	15	11	14	29
Total	27	30	37	34	31	50

Environmental Parameters

Slight differences in environmental conditions among sampling periods on the six occasions were noticeable (Table 17.3). The highest and lowest soil relative humidity were recorded on February and June visits, respectively.

Aspects of the Ecology of A. Simoni

The sampling methods varied in effectiveness in catching *A. simoni* workers, between transects and between times of year. No sampling method was effective in attracting these workers on all occasions. The species was recorded in all months at

Table 17.3: Environmental parameters of Gilimale Forest recorded on each occasion in 2004 (mean of ten measurements ± SD)

Parameter	Feb	Apr	Jun	Aug	Oct	Dec
Air temperature (°C)	27.0 ± 2.8	29.1 ± 1.2	26.0 ± 1.3	28.5 ± 2.0	27.6 ± 1.7	27.5 ± 2.5
Soil temperature (°C)	24.6 ± 1.3	26.5 ± 0.53	24.4 ± 0.53	26.0 ± 1.7	26.3 ± 1.8	25.3 ± 2.1
Mean litter depth (cm)	2.3 ± 0.89	4.7 ± 1.7	5.3 ± 0.44	3.9 ± 0.2	4.6 ± 1.0	2.6 ± 1.1
Soil humidity (%)	35.7 ± 2.2	32.1 ± 1.4	19.6 ± 0.19	23.3 ± 4.6	28.0 ± 2.1	33.0 ± 4.1

Transects 2, 3, 4, 5 and 7, and in all, except December, at Transects 1, 6 and 9. Percentage frequency of occurrence [(Number of transects positive for *A. simoni* / 10) × 100] of this species in Gilimale Forest ranged from 80% to 90% on the six occasions. The relative abundance of workers ranged from 3% to 6% of all collected specimens, with the highest proportion in February. Table 17.4 shows that all methods except the tree traps were effective for detecting this species on each occasion.

DISCUSSION

Twelve subfamilies of ants have been recorded from Sri Lankaand all but Ectatomminae were observed during this survey. Aneuretinae, Dolichoderinae, Formicinae, Myrmicinae and Ponerinae were observed throughout the study period.

Two subfamilies more rarely encountered in Sri Lanka, Cerapachyinae (detected only from soil sifting, Table 17.4) and Dorylinae (detected only from canned fish baits, soil sifting and hand collection, Table 17.4), were detected on single occasions, and Aenictinae, Amblyoponinae and Leptanillinae were observed on three to four visits (Table 13.1), probably due to their cryptic habit and lower effectiveness of these methods. All five ant subfamilies recorded from this forest, Aneuretinae, Dolichoderinae, Formicinae, Myrmicinae and Ponerinae (according to current classification), were recorded during the present survey.

Sixty-two genera of ants have been recorded from Sri Lanka and 38 of those were recorded from Gilimale Forest in 2004, indicating a high diversity of ants in this wet zone forest. This is the only survey of ants that has been conducted in Gilimale Forest recently using several sampling methods simultaneously and also with repeated sampling. Higher species richness was revealed by the simultaneous application of several sampling methods, as observed in other ant research conducted in Sri Lanka and elsewhere.

Table 17.5: Effective Sampling Method/s for each Species

Ant species	Effective methods
Aenictus sp.	LS, SS, HC
Amblyopone sp.	LS, SS
Aneuretus simoni	CB, HB, LS, SS, HC, WM, PT
Cerapachys sp.	SS
Dorylus sp.	CB, SS, HC
Dolichoderus sp. 1	CB, HB, LS, HC, PT, TT
Tapinoma indicum	CB, HB, LS, SS, HC, PT
T. melanocephalum	CB, HB, SS, TT
Technomyrmex bicolor	CB, HB, LS, SS, HC, WM, PT, TT
T. albipes	CB, HB, LS, SS, HC, PT, TT
Acropyga acutiventris	SS
Anoplolepis gracilipes	CB, HB
Camponotus sp. 1	CB, HB, LS, HC, WM, PT, TT
C. sp. 2	CB, HB, LS, HC, WM, PT, TT
Lepisiota sp.	LS, SS
Myrmoteras sp.	LS, SS
*Paratrechina** sp.	CB, HB, LS, HC, WM, PT, TT
P. longicornis	LS, SS
Polyrhachis sp.	CB, HB, SS, HC
Pseudolasius sp.	SS
Leptanilla sp.	LS, SS
Calyptomyrmex sp.	SS, PT
Cardiocondyla sp.	SS
Carebara sp.	CB, HB, LS, SS, HC, WM
Cataulacus sp.	HC
Crematogaster sp. 1	CB, HB, LS, HC, PT, TT
C. sp. 2	CB, HB, LS, HC
C. sp. 3	CB, HB
Lophomyrmex quadrispinosus	CB, HB, LS, HC
Meranoplus bicolor	HB, LS, PT
Monomorium sp.	HB, LS, WM

Ant species	Effective methods
Myrmicaria brunnea	CB, HB, LS, SS, HC, WM, PT, TT
Pheidole sp. 2	CB, HB, LS, SS, HC, WM, PT
P. sp. 7	CB, HB, LS, SS, HC, WM, PT
P. sp. 8	CB, HB, LS, SS, HC, WM, PT
Pheidologeton sp.	CB, HB, LS, SS, WM, PT
Solenopsis sp.	CB, HB, LS, SS, HC, WM, PT
Strumigenys (Quadristruma) sp.	LS, HC, WM
Tetramorium sp.	CB, HB, LS, HC, PT
T. bicarinatum	CB, HB, LS, SS, HC, WM, PT
Anochetus sp.	HB, LS, SS, HC
Centromyrmex feae	LS, SS
Hypoponera sp.	LS, SS
Leptogenys sp.	HB, LS, SS, HC, PT
Odontomachus simillimus	CB, HB, LS, SS, HC, PT
Ponera sp.	CB, HB, LS, SS, HC, PT
Pachycondyla sp. 1	LS
P. sp. 2	HC
P. sp. 3	LS, SS
Tetraponera allaborans	LS, HC

CB = Canned-fish Bait, HB = Honey Bait, HC = Hand Collection, LS = Litter Sieving, PT = Pitfall Trapping, SS = Soil Sieving, WM = Mini-Winkler extraction, TT = Tree traps

All ant genera reported previously at Gilimale were collected during this survey. In addition to the 11 ant genera reported, this study recorded 26 additional genera from the Gilimale Forest. *Pheidole, Monomorium, Tetramorium* and *Paratrechina* were reported from this forest and were also observed in Table 17.1. Other ant genera associated with *A. simoni* in "Pompekelle," Ratnapura (another habitat of this species) in May 2001, *Anoplolepis, Cataulacus, Crematogaster, Pachycondyla, Pheidole, Pheidologeton, Solenopsis* and *Tetramorium* (Dias 2004), were also observed in the present collection. The results of the present survey suggest this forest reserve has continuously been a habitat of *A. simoni* from 1955 (Wilson *et al.* 1956) to 2004. It appears that environmental conditions such as soil temperature (24°C to 28°C in 2004) and soil humidity (19.6% to 35.7% in 2004) are favourable for this rare and endemic ant species when compared with those at a dry-zone forest (soil temperature: 30.6°C to 31.1°C; soil humidity 4.8% to 6.4%) where this ant was absent.

The use of honey baits in daytime and leaf-litter sifting resulted in finding the workers of this species more often than the other methods. Although overall relative abundance seemed to be low, this species made up a considerable proportion of individuals of this ant community. However, this compound measure of abundance is influenced by the effectiveness of each method in detecting each species, and gives only an indication of actual relative abundance.

The species recorded in Table 17.1 can be considered a preliminary inventory of the ants of Gilimale Forest Reserve, and the list can doubtless be extended. But it serves as a reference for ant researchers and ecologists. Clearing of this forest for cultivation or development should be prohibited; as such actions may affect the existing favourable conditions for this evolutionarily-important ant species as well as for other rare ant species such as *Aenictus* sp., *Amblyopone* sp., *Cerapachys* sp., *Dorylus* sp., *Leptanilla* sp. and *Cardiocondyla* sp. Further ant surveys are recommended to improve the current inventory and to investigate the nesting ecology of *A. simoni*.

Glossary

abdomen — The posterior body division of an arthropod.

abiotic disease — A disease caused by factors other than pathogens.

abiotic disorder — A disease caused by factors other than a pathogen; physiological disorder.

achene — A simple, one-seeded fruit in which the seed is attached to the ovary wall at only one point, such as the "seed" on the surface of a strawberry.

adventitious — A structure arising from an unusual place, such as roots growing from leaves or stems.

aestivation — A state of inactivity during the summer months.

albedo — White, spongy inner part of citrus fruit rind.

alkaline — Basic, having a pH greater than 7.

allelopathy — The ability of a plant species to produce substances that are toxic to certain other plants.

allowable depletion — The proportion of available water that can be used before irrigation is needed.

angular leaf spot — Bacterial blight.

annual — A plant that normally completes its life cycle of seed germination, vegetative growth, reproduction, and death in a single year.

antagonists — Organisms that release toxins or otherwise change conditions so that activity or growth of other organisms (especially pests) is reduced.

antenna (pl: antennae) — The paired segmented sensory organs, borne one on each side of the head, commonly termed horns or feelers.

anthers — The pollen-producing organs of flowers.

anticoagulant — A substance that prevents blood clotting, resulting in internal hemorrhaging; may be used as a rodenticide.

apical dominance — Growth of the bud at the apex of a stem or tuber while growth of all other buds on the stem or tuber is inhibited.

apothecia — Cup-shaped, spore-bearing structures produced by certain types of fungi such as Sclerotinia.

ascospores — A spore produced within the saclike cell of the sexual state of a fungus.

auricle — A small earlike projection from the base of a leaf or petal.

available water — The amount of water held in the soil that can be extracted by plants.

awn — A slender bristlelike organ usually at the apex of a plant structure.

axil — The upper angle between a twig or leaf and the stem from which it is growing.

axillary bud A bud formed in an axil.

B.t. Abbreviation for *Bacillus thuringiensis.*

Bacillus thuringiensis A bacterium that causes disease in many insects, especially caterpillars; formulations of the bacteria are used as insecticides.

bacterium/bacteria A single-celled, microscopic, plantlike organism that lacks a nucleus. Most bacteria obtain their nitrogen and energy from organic matter; some bacteria cause plant or animal diseases.

band application An application in which a material such as fertilizer or herbicide is applied in strips, usually to the bed or seed row.

basin A portion of a rice field bounded by levees.

beneficials Organisms that provide a benefit to crop production, applied especially to natural enemies of pests and to pollinators such as bees.

biennial A plant that completes its life cycle in two years and usually does not flower until the second season.

binomial sampling A sampling method that involves recording only the presence or absence of members of the population being sampled (such as an insect pest) on a sample unit (such as a leaf), rather than counting the numbers of individuals; presence/absence sampling.

biodegradation The breaking down of a chemical by organisms in the environment.

biofix	An identifiable event that signals when to begin degree-day accumulation.
biological control	The action of parasites, predators, or pathogens in maintaining another organism's population density at a lower average level than would occur in their absence. Biological control may occur naturally in the field or result from manipulation or introduction of biological control agents by people.
biotic disease	Disease caused by a pathogen, such as a bacterium, fungus, mycoplasma, or virus.
biotype	A strain of a species that has certain biological characters separating it from other individuals of that species.
blackarm	Bacterial blight lesions on stems.
blank	Nut with no kernel-consists of only the collapsed pellicle (skin).
blanking	Producing no grain or seed (used to describe individual florets of the rice panicle).
blight	A disease characterized by general and rapid killing of leaves, flowers, and branches.
blind node	The first node formed on a strawberry runner that usually does not form a daughter plant.
bolt	To initiate the growth of flower structures.
boot	A bulge in the upper leaf sheath caused by the expansion of the developing panicle.

bordeaux mixture A fungicide made of a mixture of hydrated lime and copper sulfate.

border harvesting A harvesting method that leaves a strip of uncut hay along every other border; next harvest these borders are mowed and the alternate borders are left standing.

borrow pits Depressions on either side of a levee created when soil is removed from the field to build the levee.

botanical Derived from plants or plant parts.

bract A modified leaf at the base of a flower.

broad-spectrum pesticide A pesticide that kills a large number of unrelated species.

broadcast application The application of a material such as fertilizer or herbicide to the entire surface of a field.

brood All the individuals of a generation that hatch at about the same time.

bud Bud that forms in the axil of a leaf.

bulb An underground storage organ, composed chiefly of enlarged, fleshy leaf bases.

calcareous soil Doil containing high levels of calcium carbonate.

calibrate To standardize or correct the measuring devices on instruments; to adjust nozzles on a spray rig properly.

calyx The sepals of a flower; they enclose the unopened flower bud.

cambium Thin layer of undifferentiated, actively

	growing tissue between phloem and xylem.
canker	A dead, discolored, often sunken area (lesion) on a root, trunk, stem, or branch.
canopy	The leafy parts of vines or trees.
carcinogen	A substance or agent capable of causing cancer.
caterpillar	The larva of a butterfly, moth, sawfly, or scorpionfly.
catfacing	Disfigurement or malformation of fruit; in the case of strawberries, usually the result of injury to developing achenes by Lygus bugs or low temperature.
catkin	A spikelike cluster of unisexual flowers, e.g., the male flowers of walnut.
cauda	A process resembling a tail.
certified seed or planting stock	Seeds, tubers or young plants certified by a recognized authority to be free of or to contain less than a minimum number of specified pests or pathogens.
certified transplants	Strawberry plants that have received a certification tag from the California Department of Food and Agriculture, production practices must meet standards for freedom from pest problems and plant samples from production fields must test free of viruses.
check	The part of a rice field between two levees.
chilling	In strawberries, exposure to

temperatures low enough to induce the production of food reserves needed to support vigorous vegetative growth.

chlamydospore Thick-walled spore formed from the cell of a fungus hypha.

chlorophyll The green pigment of plants that captures the energy from sunlight necessary for photosynthesis.

chlorosis Yellowing or bleaching of normally green plant tissue usually caused by the loss of chlorophyll.

chorion The outer membrane of an insect egg.

circulative virus A virus that systemically infects its insect vector and usually is transmitted for the remainder of the vector's life; persistent virus.

cocoon A sheath, usually of silk, formed by an insect larva as a chamber for pupation.

cohort A group.

cole crops Any of the group of crucifer family crops that are varieties of the species Brassica oleracea, including cabbage, broccoli, cauliflower, and brussel spouts.

coleoptile A sheathlike structure enclosing the shoot of a grass seedling.

collar region In grasses, the region where the leaf blade and sheath meet; it is used in identifying species; in trees, the trunk area at the soil line.

companion planting The practice of planting certain plant species-often herbs-in close association with crop plants to repel pests.

competitive exclusion agent Organism capable of outcompeting other organisms, thus excluding them from the environment.

conidium (pl: conidia) A type of asexual fungal spore.

control action guideline A guideline used to determine if pest control action is needed.

control action threshold Pest population level at which treatment is necessary to prevent economic loss, also called economic threshold.

cornicle Two tubular structures located on the posterior part of an aphid's abdomen.

cortex Tissue between the phloem and the epidermis in roots and stems.

cotyledon A leaf formed within the seed and present on a seedling at germination; seed leaf.

cover crops Cultivation of a second type of crop primarily to improve the production system for a primary crop; examples include grasses or legumes maintained in orchards or vineyards and legume or other crops grown during the winter season to improve soil condition.

crawler The active first instar of a scale insect.

crochets Tiny hooks on the prolegs of caterpillars.

cross resistance In pest management, resistance of a pest population to a pesticide to which it has not been exposed that accompanies the development of

	resistance to a pesticide to which it has been exposed.
crown	The part of the alfalfa plant from which new shoots are produced, emerging at soil surface just above taproot; the point at or just below the soil surface where the main stem (trunk) and roots join. Also used to refer to the topmost limbs on a tree or shrub; the shortened stem of a strawberry plant, from which roots, leaves, and fruit trusses arise.
culm	The jointed stem of grasses.
cultivar	A specially developed agricultural plant variety.
curing	Holding potato tubers under warm, humid conditions that favor wound healing.
cutout	A period of reduced growth and square production following a fruiting cycle.
damping-off	Destruction of seedlings by one or a combination of pathogens that weaken the stem or root.
daughter plants	Vegetative progeny of strawberry plants; plants that develop along the runners produced by another strawberry plant called the mother plant.
day-neutral	The term applied to strawberry cultivars that produce flower buds more or less independently of day length; everbearing.
degree-day	A unit combining temperature and time used in monitoring growth and development of organisms.

dehiscence Opening naturally and regularly along lines of weakness; in fruits, opening along sutures to release seeds.

delayed dormant Refers to the treatment period in fruit tree crops, beginning when buds begin to swell until the beginning of green tip development.

determinate Having stems and branches that stop growing at a certain point, usually after producing flowers. In cotton, this term is applied to varieties with a distinct interruption in growth following fruit set.

developmental threshold The lowest temperature at which growth occurs in a given species.

diapause A period of physiologically controlled dormancy in insects.

disease Any disturbance of a plant that interferes with its normal structure, function, or economic value.

disk A type of cultivator made up of many circular blades used for weed control and soil preparation.

dormant To become inactive during winter or periods of cold weather.

dough stage A stage in grain development when the grain turns from a liquid to a soft doughy consistency before hardening.

drag off The practice of removing soil from the tops of potato hills before sprout emergence.

drift The aerial dispersal of a substance such as a pesticide beyond the intended application area.

DTPA A chemical solution used to determine available zinc in the soil: [[(carboxymethyl) imino] bis (ethyleneitrilo)l tetra-acetic acid.

dwarfing A stunting of normal growth characterized in plants by smaller than normal leaves and stems.

economic threshold A level of pest population or damage at which the cost of control action equals the crop value gained from control action.

ectoparasite A parasite that lives on the outside of its host.

embryo The small plantlet within the seeds in almond, the embryo develops into the kernel.

endoparasite A parasite that lives inside its host.

endosperm The tissue containing stored food in a seed that surrounds the embryo and is eventually digested by the embryo as it grows.

English walnut The walnut species (*Juglans regia)* used for the selection of commercial scion cultivars; origin believed in Persia (= Persian walnut).

entomophagous nematodes Nematodes that eat insects.

epicotyl The part of an embryo or seedling above the attachment point of the cotyledon(s).

epidermis The outermost layer of living cells on the surface of a plant or animal.

evapotranspiration The loss of soil moisture due to evaporation from the soil surface and transpiration by plants.

everbearing Term applied to strawberry cultivars that produce flowers and fruit all year as long as temperatures are favorable; often used synonymously with day-neutral.

exclusion Keeping a pest and crop separate from one another.

extrafloral nectary A nectary located outside the flower.

eye A collection of several buds on the surface of a potato tuber, one of which will sprout and form a new stem when conditions are favorable.

fallow Cultivated land that is allowed to lie dormant, with no crops growing on it, during a growing season.

feeder roots The youngest roots with root hairs, important in absorption of water and minerals.

field capacity The moisture level in soil after saturation and runoff.

flag leaf The terminal leaf of a grass plant; the last emerging leaf below the grain head.

flavedo Outer part of the rind of citrus fruit, bearing oil glands and pigments.

flight Period of flying activity of moths from one generation.

floret An individual flower in a grass spikelet.

flower bud A bud in which flower parts are contained.

frass Solid fecal material produced by insects.

fruiting bodies In fungi, reproductive structures containing spores.

fumigation Treatment with a pesticide active ingredient that is a gas under treatment conditions.

fungicide A pesticide used for control of fungi.

fungus (pl: fungi) A multicellular lower plant lacking chlorophyll, such as mold, mildew, smut, or rust. The fungus body normally consists of filamentous strands called mycelium and reproduces through dispersal of spores.

gall Localized swelling or outgrowth of plant tissue, often formed in response to the action of a pathogen or other pest.

girdle Damage that completely encircles a stem or root, often resulting in death of plant parts above or below the girdle.

glume The outer brack of a grass spikelet.

glycoalkaloid A bitter-tasting compound present in potato foliage and in the epidermis of potato tubers.

gossypol A substance poisonous to many animals, produced by numerous small glands in most cotton varieties.

graft union Place where the rootstock joins the scion or top part of a grafted tree or vine.

ground cover Any of various low, dense-growing plants, as ivy, pachysandra, etc., used for covering the ground, as in places where it is difficult to grow grass.

head The inflorescence of many grass plants, including small grains.

heat unit Synonym for degree-day.

herbicide A pesticide used to control weeds.

hibernaculum (plural: hibernacula) A shelter occupied during the winter by an insect, notably peach twig borer.

honeydew An excretion from insects, such as aphids, mealybugs, whiteflies, and soft scales, consisting of modified plant sap.

horticultural oils Highly refined petroleum (or seed derived) oils that are manufactured specifically to control pests on plants.

host A plant or animal that provides sustenance for another organism.

hypha (pl.: hyphae) One of the filaments forming the body, or mycelium, of a fungus.

hypocotyl The portion of an embryo or seedling between the cotyledons and the developing root tip.

immune Exempt from infection by a given pathogen.

incorporate To mix a material such as an herbicide into the soil by mechanical action.

indeterminate Having a growth pattern in which stems continue growing indefinitely; with flower clusters, the opening of the lower (lateral) flowers first, and the terminal one opening later.

indexing Testing a plant for a virus infection, usually by grafting tissue from it onto an indicator plant.

infection The entry of a pathogen into a host and establishment of the pathogen as a parasite of the host.

infestation The presence of a large number of pest organisms in an area or field, on the surface of a host or anything that might contact a host, or in the soil.

inflorescence Ilower cluster.

inner bark In older trees, the living part of the bark, the phloem.

inoculum Any part or stage of a pathogen, such as spores or virus particles, that can infect a host.

inorganic Containing no carbon; generally used to indicate materials (for example, fertilizers) that are of mineral origin.

instar The larval or nymph stage of an immature insect between successive molts.

integrated pest management (IPM) A pest management strategy that focuses on long-term prevention or suppression of pest problems through a combination of techniques such as encouraging biological control, use of resistant varieties, and adoption of alternate cultural practices such as modification of irrigation or pruning to make the habitat less conducive to pest development Pesticides are used only when careful monitoring indicates they are needed according to preestablished

	guidelines, treatment thresholds, or to prevent pests from significantly interfering with the purposes for which plants are being grown.
internode	The portion of a stem between two nodes.
invertebrate	An animal having no internal skeleton.
jointing	Elongation of rice internodes before flowering.
June bearing	A term applied to short-day strawberry cultivars.
juvenile	Immature form of a nematode that hatches from an egg and molts several times before becoming an adult.
larva (pl.: larvae)	The immature form of insects that develop through the process of complete metamorphosis including egg, several larval stages, pupa, and adult In mites, the first-stage immature is also called a larva.
latent	Producing no visible symptoms (generally refers to an infection or a pathogen).
latent period	The time between when a vector acquires a pathogen and when the vector becomes able to transmit the pathogen to a new host; also, the time between infection of a host plant and production of inoculum by the infection.
layby application	An application, usually of fertilizer or herbicide, after the crop is well established; especially, an application at

the latest time in the season when it is still possible to pass through the field with a tractor.

leaching fraction The proportion of applied irrigation water that is added to meet the crop's leaching requirement.

leaching requirement The amount of water in excess of a crop's evapotranspiration requirement that is needed to maintain maximum yield by leaching harmful salts from the root zone.

leaf area index The ratio between the total leaf surface area of a plant and the surface area of ground that is covered by the plant.

leaf margin The outer edge of the leaf; leaf margins may be smooth, lobed, indented, etc.

lenticels Natural openings in the surface of a tuber or stem, similar to leaf stomata, that can open and close and allow gas exchange.

lepidopterous Of or pertaining to the Order Lepidoptera, the moths and butterflys.

lesion Localized area of diseased or discolored tissue.

ligule In many grasses, a short membranous projection on the inner side of the leaf blade at the junction where the leaf blade and leaf sheath meet.

locule One of the seed chambers in the ovary or boll.

lodging The toppling of plants of a grain crop before harvest, often from wind, rain, or waterfowl.

mandibles	Jaws; the forward-most pair of mouthparts of an insect.
meconium	Fecal pellet excreted by a larva before pupation.
meristem	The collection of cells at the growing point of a plant that are capable of cell division.
metamorphosis	The change in form that takes place as insects grow from immatures to adults.
microbial pesticides	Pesticides that consist of bacteria, fungi, viruses, or other microorganisms used for control of weeds, invertebrates, or plant pathogens
microorganism	An organism of microscopic size, such as a bacterium, virus, fungus, viroid, or mycoplasma.
micropropagation	Generation of new, disease-free potato plants from tiny pieces of meristem tissue.
microsclerotia (sin.: microsclerotium)	Very small sclerotia, such as those produced by the Verticillium wilt fungus.
milk stage	The early stage of grain development when the grain is filled with a milky liquid.
mineral oils	Synonymous with horticultural oils.
minituber	A small tuber produced under greenhouse conditions on a small potato plant generated by micropropagation.
modify environmental factors	Factors such as moisture and heat, and, in the case of certain organic materials that decay, to gradually improve soil

quality. Plant derived in (organic) or synthetic materials may be used.

molt In insects and other arthropods, the shedding of skin before entering another stage of growth.

monitoring Carefully watching and recording information on the activities, growth, development, and abundance of organisms or other factors on a regular basis over a period of time, often utilizing very specific procedures.

mulch A layer of material placed on the soil surface to prevent weed growth.

mummy Unharvested nut remaining on the tree (also called sticktight); the crusty skin of an aphid whose inside has been consumed by a parasite.

mutation The abrupt appearance of a new, heritable characteristic as the result of a change in the genetic material of one individual cell.

mycelium (pl.: mycelia) The vegetative body of a fungus, consisting of a mass of slender filaments called hyphae.

mycoplasma A member of the genus Mycoplasma. Mycoplasmas, unlike viruses, can reproduce in the absence of a host and are the smallest free-living organisms; they have a unit membrane but no cell wall as do bacteria.

mycorrhizae Beneficial associations between plant roots and fungi.

narrow-range oil A highly refined petroleum or seed-derived oil that is manufactured specifically to control pests on plants, also called horticultural oil.

natural enemies Predators, parasites, or pathogens that are considered beneficial because they attack and kill organisms that we normally consider to be pests.

necrosis Death of tissue accompanied by dark brown discoloration, usually occurring in a well-defined part of a plant, such as the portion of a leaf between leaf veins or the xylem or phloem in a stem or tuber.

nectary A gland that secretes nectar.

nodes The leafbearing joints on plant stems.

nonpersistent virus A virus that is carried on the mouthparts of its insect vector and is lost after the vector feeds once or a few times; styletborne virus.

nucellus In plants, the watery tissue composing the chief part of the young ovule in the flower and inside the seed during early development. It furnishes nutrients to the young embryo and is digested by the developing endosperm and embryo.

nymph The immature stage of insects such as grasshoppers and aphids, that hatch from eggs and gradually acquire adult form through a series of molts without passing through a pupal stage.

organic A material (e.g. pesticide) whose molecules contain carbon and hydrogen atoms. Also may refer to plants or animals which are grown without the use of synthetic fertilizers or pesticides.

outer bark In older trees, the dead part of the bark.

oviposit To lay or deposit eggs.

oviposition The laying or depositing of eggs.

packing tissue Firm, membranous tissue lining the walnut shell and separating the kernel halves.

panicle A branching cluster of flowers held on a stem, such as the flowering parts of most grasses.

pappus The modified calyx of flowers in the sunflower family; usually takes the form of bristles, scales, or awns.

parasite An organism that derives its food from the body of another organism, the host, without killing the host directly; also an insect that spends its immature stages in the body of a host that dies just before the parasite emerges (this type is also called a parasitoid).

parthenocarpy Development of fruit without fertilization and seed.

parthenogenesis Development of an egg without fertilization.

pathogen A disease-causing organism.

peduncle The stem of an individual flower or fruit.

peg roots Primary roots.

pellicle The covering (skin) that encloses the kernel; it is white during development but becomes brown at maturity.

perennial A plant that can live three or more years and flower at least twice.

periderm Several layers of corky cells located on the outside of the epidermis of a potato tuber and containing high amounts of suberin.

perithecium (plural: perithecia) A globular to flask-shaped fruiting body that has an apical pore through which the spores (ascospores) are released.

persistent virus A virus that systemically infects its insect vector and usually is transmitted for the remainder of the vector's life.

pest resurgence The rapid rebound of a pest population after it has been controlled.

pesticide Any substance or mixture intended for preventing, destroying, repelling, killing, or mitigating problems caused by any insects, rodents, weeds, nematodes, fungi, or other pests; and any other substance or mixture intended for use as a plant growth regulator, defoliant, or desiccant.

pesticide resistance The genetically acquired ability of an organism to survive a pesticide application at doses that once killed most individuals of the same species.

petiole The stalk connecting the leaf to a stem.

pH A value used to express relative acidity or alkalinity.

phenoxy herbicides A group of herbicides derived from phenoxy-acetic acid, including 2,4-D, 2,4,5-T, 2,4-DB, MCPA and silvex.

pheromone A substance secreted by an organism to affect the behavior or development of other members of the same species; sex pheromones that attract the opposite sex for mating are used in monitoring certain insects.

phloem The food-conducting tissue of a plant, made up of sieve tubes, companion cells, phloem parenchyma, and fibers.

phloem-feeding An organism that withdraws nutrients from the food-conducting tissue of a plant's vascular system.

photosynthate The products of photosynthesis, used to support growth, respiration, and fruit production.

photosynthesis The process by which plants convert sunlight into energy.

physiological disorder A disorder caused by factors other than a pathogen; abiotic disorder.

phytotoxicity The ability of a material such as a pesticide or fertilizer to cause injury to plants.

pinhead square A square approximately 1/8 inch (3mm) or less in length.

pistil Female part of the flower, usually consisting of ovules, ovary, style, and stigma.

pollinator The agent of pollen transfer, usually bees.

pollinizer The producer of pollen; the variety used as a source of pollen for cross-pollination.

pome fruit A simple fleshy fruit, the outer portion of which is formed by the floral parts that surround the ovary.

postemergence herbicide Herbicide applied after the emergence of weeds.

predator Any animal (including insects and mites) that kills other animals (prey) and feeds on them.

preemergence herbicide Herbicide applied before emergence of weeds.

primary bloom The first production of flowers on a potato plant, occurring after 8 to 12 leaves have been formed on the mainstem and generally coinciding with the beginning of the tuber growth phase.

primary inoculum The initial source of a pathogen that starts disease development in a given location.

primary roots Roots that develop from the crown of a strawberry plant.

proleg A fleshy, unsegmented leg of caterpillars.

propagules Any part of a plant from which a new plant can grow, including seeds, bulbs, rootstocks, etc.

protectant fungicide Fungicide that protects a plant from infection by a pathogen.

protective coverings Any cloth, screen, plastic or other material placed over growing plants to

	prevent damage by pests or harsh weather.
prothorax	The anterior of the three thoracic segments of an insect.
pupa	The nonfeeding, inactive stage between larva and adult in insects with complete metamorphosis.
pupate	To molt from the larval stage to the pupa.
pustule	Small blisterlike elevation of epidermis from which spores emerge.
pycnidium (plural: pycnidia)	Small, spherical or flask-shaped structure, formed by certain types of fungi, inside which spores are produced.
quadrant	One of four equal parts into which a field is divided for monitoring.
quarantine	A period of enforced isolation that is required to prevent movement of undesireable organisms.
random sample	A sampling plan in which locations for samples are not predetermined either by previous sampling in that field or the relationship of one sample site to another.
rat-tail bloom	A secondary bloom in Bartlett pears that results when terminal buds form and open on the current season's growth.
receptacle	The apex of the flower stem that bears the organs of the flower.
regrowth bud	The buds on alfalfa crowns that become new stems.

reproductive bud	The buds on alfalfa stems that become flowers.
reservoir	The site where a pest population or quantity of inoculum can survive in the absence of a host crop, and from which a new crop may be invaded.
residue management	Management of rice straw and stubble after harvest.
resistant	Able to tolerate conditions (such as pesticide sprays or pest damage) harmful to other strains of the same species.
respiration	The process by which nutrients are metabolized to provide energy needed for cellular activity.
rhizome	A horizontal, underground shoot, especially one that forms roots at the nodes to produce new plants.
rogue	To remove diseased plants from a field.
rolling	Mechanical crushing of potato vines to hasten vine death, sometimes used synonymously with vine-killing.
rootstock	An underground stem or rhizome; lower portion of a graft which develops into the root system.
rosette	A cluster of leaves arranged in a compact circular pattern, often at a shoot tip or on a shortened stem.
rosetted bloom	A flower whose petals have been tied together with silk by a pink bollworm larva.
rosetting	Abnormal growth caused by certain pathogens in which new potato foliage is stunted and tightly bunched.

rotation The practice of purposefully alternating crop species grown on the same plot of land.

row covers Any fabric or protective covering placed over rows of plants to protect them from pest damage or harsh climate.

rue leaf Any leaf produced after the seed leaves (cotyledons).

rugose A rough appearance of leaves in which veins are sunken and interveinal tissue raised, caused by certain virus infections.

ruminant Any of the hoofed mammals (including cattle, deer, sheep) that chew the cud.

runner Stolon of a strawberry plant, on which a daughter plant may develop.

russeting Thickening of the periderm on tubers of russet cultivars that occurs after vine senescence.

sanitation Any activity that reduces the spread of pathogen inoculum, such as removal and destruction of infected plant parts, cleaning of tools and field equipment.

scion The portion above a graft that becomes the trunk, branch, and tree top; the cultivar or variety.

sclerotium (pl.: sclerotia) A compact mass of hardened mycelium that serves as a dormant stage in some fungi.

secondary bloom A second production of flowers on a potato plant, occurring at the end of the mainstem of an indeterminate cultivar;

secondary bloom may occur on a determinate cultivar at leaf axils along the mainstem.

secondary infection Infection by microorganisms that enter the host through an injury caused previously by another pathogen.

secondary outbreak The increase of a nontarget pest to harmful levels following a pesticide application, caused by destruction of natural enemies that normally control the nontarget pest.

secondary roots The network of fine roots that develops from the primary roots of a strawberry plant and picks up water and nutrients from the soil; white roots.

secondary spread The spread of a pathogen within a field after the initial or primary infection.

secondary stems Stems formed by stolons that emerge from the soil.

sedges A group of grasslike, herbaceous plants that, unlike grasses, have unjointed stems. Stems are usually solid and often triangular in cross section.

seed leaf The leaf formed in a seed and present on a seedling at germination; cotyledon.

seed piece Portion of a potato tuber containing at least one eye that is planted to produce a new potato plant.

seedcotton Harvested lint that is still attached to seeds; i.e., the lint before ginning.

selective pesticide Pesticides that are toxic primarily to the target pest (and perhaps a few related

	species), leaving most other organisms, including natural enemies, unharmed.
self fruitful	The ability to set fruit with pollen from the same flower or tree.
senescence	The stage of growth in a plant or plant part from maturity to death, characterized by an accumulation of metabolic products, an increased respiratory rate, and a loss in dry weight.
sepal	One of the outermost flower structures which usually enclose the other flower parts in the bud.
sequential sampling	A sampling method in which the number of samples is not fixed in advance.
sessile	Attached or fastened, incapable of moving from place to place; attached directly without a stem.
seta (plural: setae)	A bristle.
sheath	The part of a grass leaf that encloses the stem below the collar region.
short day	Term applied to strawberry cultivars that require a period of time with day length shorter than a minimum (about 14 hours) for the induction of flower buds; June-bearing.
side dressing	Fertilizer or other material added to the soil around a growing crop.
sieve tubes	See phloem.
skeletonize	To remove leaf tissue between the veins, leaving the network of veins intact.

soil profile A vertical section of the soil through all its horizontal layers, extending into the parent material.

solarization The practice of heating soil to levels lethal to pests through application of clear plastic to the soil surface for 4 to 6 weeks during sunny, warm weather.

sooty mold A sooty coating on foliage or fruit, formed by the dark mycelia of fungi that live in the honeydew secreted by certain insects.

specific gravity The ratio of the density of a substance to the density of pure water; specific gravity of potato tubers is used as a measure of their dry matter content.

spikelets The collection of individual grass florets that are borne at the end of the smallest branch of the inflorescence.

spike An elongated inflorescence in which the individual flowers are borne tightly against the main stem or rachis.

spiracle An external opening of the system of ducts, or tracheae, that serves as a respiratory system in insects.

sporangium (plural: sporangia) A structure in which asexual spores are produced.

spore A reproductive body produced by certain fungi and other organisms, capable of growing into a new individual under proper conditions.

sporulation The production of spores.

spraing (sprain) Reddish brown spots, rings, or arcs in tuber tissue caused by tobacco rattle virus; corky ringspot.

sprout	The new stem formed from the eye of a potato tuber.
sprout inhibitor	A chemical applied to potato vines or to stored tubers to prevent sprouting.
spur	Short woody shoot that is the primary fruiting structure for most fruit trees.
square	A cotton flower bud.
staminate flower	A male flower.
stand decline	The gradual (over a period of 3-5 years) debilitation of the plants in an alfalfa field caused by the combined effects of pests and unfavorable environmental conditions.
stand establishment in an alfalfa field	The period of plant establishment between planting and first cutting.
stele	The central cylinder inside the cortex of the roots and stems of vascular plants; contains the vascular or conducting tissue.
sticktight	Nut that remains on the tree after harvest (also called mummy); nut with husk firmly adhering to shell.
stipe	A stalk.
stolon	A trailing aboveground stem or shoot, often rooting at the nodes and forming new plants.
stoma (pl.: stomata)	Natural opening in a leaf surface that serves for gas exchange and water evaporation and has the ability to open and close in response to environmental conditions.

stroma A compact, usually spore-producing structure formed from fungal mycelium on the surface of a host.

stub cotton A cotton crop in which the stalks are cut down after harvest but the crown and rootstock are left in the ground to regrow the following season.

styletborne virus A virus that is carried on the mouthparts of its insect vector and is lost after the vector feeds once or a few times; nonpersistent virus.

suberin A waxy substance, resistant to microbial attack, formed in the corky cells of periderm layers.

suberization The formation of periderm layers on the cut surfaces or wounds of potato tubers.

substituted dinitroanilines A class of herbicides widely used for preplant application in cotton.

sucker Shoot arising from the trunk or rootstock.

summer planting A system of strawberry culture in which planting occurs in summer and fruit production begins the following spring.

sun checking Cracking or breaking of whole kernels of grain caused by exposure to alternating conditions of dew, sun, and water stress.

suture Visible seam on hull.

synthetic organic pesticides Manufactured pesticides produced from petroleum and containing largely carbon and hydrogen atoms in their basic structure.

systemic Capable of moving throughout a plant or other organism, usually in the vascular system.

tail water Irrigation water that has drained from a field.

taproot The large primary root that grows vertically downward, giving off small lateral roots.

target pest A pest species that a control action is intended to destroy.

teliospore Thick-walled dark spore of rust and smut fungi that is able to survive adverse conditions.

tensiometer A device for measuring soil moisture, consisting of a buried tube of water that develops a partial vacuum as surrounding soil dries out.

terminal The growing tip of a stem, especially the main stem.

terminal spikelet stage Stage in the development of the wheat spike when the primordia of the terminal spikelet are formed.

terrestrial biotype A strain of an organism adapted to growing on land rather than in water.

tertiary bloom The third production of flowers that occurs at the end of the growing stem of an indeterminate potato cultivar.

tertiary tiller Branch of a grass plant that develops from the axil of a secondary tiller.

thorax The second of three major divisions in the body of an insect, and the one bearing the legs and wings.

thurberia weevil A race of the boll weevil that feeds on wild cotton.

tiller Branch stem of a grass plant.

tolerance Inherent lack of susceptibility to a pesticide. Also, the ability of a plant to grow in spite of infection by a pathogen.

tolerance level Maximum percentage of a disease or pest symptom allowed during field inspections for certification of a seed lot; levels are different with each field generation and may vary from state to state.

top crop Fruit produced in the second fruiting cycle of cotton, mainly on upper branches.

toxin A poisonous substance produced by a living organism.

translocated herbicide Herbicide that is able to move throughout a plant after being applied to leaf surfaces.

transpiration The evaporation of water vapor from plants, mostly through stomata.

trap crop A crop or portion of a crop intended to attract pests so they can be destroyed by treating a relatively small area or by destroying the trap crop and the pests together.

treatment threshold The level of pest population at which a pesticide or other control measure is needed to prevent eventual economic injury to the crop.

true leaf Any leaf produced after the cotyledons.

tuber An enlarged, fleshy, underground stem with buds capable of producing new plants.

tuberization The formation of tubers at the ends of stolons; tuber initiation.

unfurled Unopened.

urediospore Spore produced by a rust fungus that spreads the infection to other hosts.

variety An identifiable strain within a species, usually referring to a strain which arises in nature as opposed to a cultivar which is specifically bred for particular properties; sometimes used synonymously with cultivar.

vascular ring A thin area of potato tuber tissue between the cortex and the medulla in which vascular tissue is concentrated.

vascular system The system of plant tissues that conducts water, mineral nutrients, and products of photosynthesis through the plant, consisting of the xylem and phloem.

vascular tissue Plant tissue that conducts water and nutrients throughout the plant.

vector An organism able to transport and transmit a pathogen to a host.

vegetative Plant parts or plant growth not involved in the production of seed, such as roots, stems, and leaves.

vein banding Dark brown discoloration of the veins on the undersides of potato leaflets caused by potato virus Y.

véraison Beginning of fruit ripening, recognized by berry softening and beginning of pigmentation in colored varieties.

vigor The capacity of a strawberry plant for active vegetative growth.

viroid A portion of infectious nucleic acid, without the protein coat of a virus.

virulence The relative infectiousness of a bacteria or virus, or its ability to overcome the resistance of the host metabolism.

virus A very small organism that can multiply only within living cells of other organisms and is capable of producing disease symptoms in some plants and animals

volunteer crop The undesired emergence of a significant stand of a self-seeded, previously planted crop in a field purposely planted with another crop.

white roots Secondary roots.

windowpane The removal of the epidermal layer of leaf tissue leaving small segments of clear tissue.

wing Extension of the nut shell at the suture line; varies in size according to cultivar.

winter planting A system of planting strawberries in mid to late fall that depends on growth during winter months for production of an early spring crop.

xanthosis A collection of symptoms consisting of distorted leaf growth and yellow leaf margins that develops in strawberry plants infected by mottle virus and

	either crinkle virus or mild yellow edge virus; yellows.
xylem	Plant tissue that conducts water and nutrients from the roots up through the plant.
Y-leaf	The most recently matured leaf.
zonate	Marked with zones or bands; belted; striped.

Bibliography

Agosti D. Revision of the ant genus *Cladomyrma*, with an outline of the higher classification of the Formicinae (Hymenoptera: Formicidae) *Systematic Entomology*. 1991; 16:293–310.

Balasubramanium S, Jayasuriya AHU, Karunaratne GPB and Dharmasena GT, 1991. *Review of Forest Management Plans for Environmental Conservation*. Unpublished final report submitted to Forestry Planning Unit, Ministry of Lands, Irrigation and Mahaweli Development.

Baroni Urbani C, Bolton B, Ward PS. The internal phylogeny of ants (Hymenoptera: Formicidae) *Systematic Entomology*. 1992; 17:301–329.

Bolton B, 1994. *Identification Guide to the Ant Genera of the World*. Harvard University Press, Cambridge, USA, 222.

Bolton B, 1995. *New General Catalogue of the Ants of the World*. Harvard University Press, USA.

Bolton B, 2003. Synopsis and classification of Formicidae. *Memoirs of the American Entomological Institute* 71:1–370.

Bolton B, Alpert G, Ward PS and Naskrecky P, 2006. *Bolton's Catalogue of Ants of the World. 1758–2005*. CD-ROM, Copyrights by Harvard University Press.

Bolton B. A new general catalogue of the ants of the world. Harvard University Press; Cambridge, Mass: 1995. p. 504.

Bolton B. *Identification guide to the ant genera of the world*. Harvard University Press; Cambridge, Mass: 1994. p. 222.

Bolton B. *Synopsis and classification of Formicidae*. Memoirs of the American Entomological Institute. 2003; 71:1–370.

Brower JE, Zar JH and Ende V, 1998. *Field and Laboratory Methods for General Ecology*. 4th edition, Wm. C. Brown Publishers, USA, 48.

Bünzli GH. *Untersuchungen über coccidophile Ameisen aus den Kaffeefelden von Surinam*. Mitteilungen der Schweizerischen Entomologischen Gesellshaft. 1935; 16:455–593.

Chenuil A, McKey DB. Molecular phylogenetic study of a myrmecophyte symbiosis: did *Leonardoxa*/ant associations diversify via cospeciation? Molecular Phylogenetics and Evolution. 1996; 6:270–286.

Currie CR, Wong B, Stuart AE, Schultz TR, Rehner SA, Mueller UG, Sung GH, Spatafora JW, Straus NA. Ancient Tripartite Coevolution in the Attine Ant-Microbe Symbiosis. *Science*. 2003; 299 (5605):386–388.

Dias RKS and Gunathilake MKCG, 2007a. Worker ant communities (Order: Hymenoptera, Family: Formicidae) of two disturbed forests in Anuradhapura district (Abstract). *Proceedings of Postgraduate Symposium of Kelaniya University* (SC/ BS/2).

Dias RKS and Gunathilake MKCG, 2007b. *Worker ant communities in two disturbed regions of Anuradhapura district (dry zone), Sri Lanka (Abstract). Proceedings of the Sixth ANeT Conference held at the University of Punjab*, Patiala, India, 6.

Dias RKS, 2004. Taxonomic key for the subfamilies of ants recorded from Sri Lanka and some information on *Aneuretus simoni* Emery in "Pompekelle," Ratnapura. *Spolia Ceylanica* 41:92–101.

Dias RKS, 2006. Current taxonomic status of ants of Sri Lanka. In: *The Fauna of Sri Lanka—Status of Taxonomy, Research and Conservation* (Bambaradeniya CNB, ed), Karunaratne and Sons Ltd. (IUCN Publication), Sri Lanka, 43–52.

Dias RKS, 2008. Amazing ants—present status of research on ants of Sri Lanka. In: *Social Insects and their Economic Importance and Conservation* (Kumarasinghe NC, ed), SLAAS and Biodiversity Secretariat of the Ministry of Environment and Natural Resources, Sri Lanka, 1–9.

Dill M, Maschwitz U. The nomadic herdsmen of Kinabalu Park: A unique lifestyle in ants. *Sabah Parks Nature Journal*. 1998; 1:61–67.

Felsenstein J. Distance methods for inferring phylogenies: a justification. *Evolution*. 1984; 38:16–24.

Flanders SE. The complete interdependence of an ant and a coccid. *Ecology*. 1957; 38:535–536.

Gaume L, Matile-Ferrero D, McKey D. Colony foundation and acquisition of coccoid trophobionts by *Aphomomyrmex afer* (Formicinae): co-dispersal of queens and phoretic mealybugs in an antplant-homopteran mutualism? *Insectes Sociaux*. 2000; 47:84–91.

Grimaldi D, Agosti D. A formicine in New Jersey Cretaceous amber (Hymenoptera: Formicidae) and early evolution of the ants. *Proceedings of the National Academy of Sciences*. 2001; 97(25):13678–13683.

Gutell RR. Collection of small subunit (16S- and 16S-like) ribosomal RNA structures. *Nucleic Acids Research*. 1994; 22:3502–3507.

Hölldobler B, Wilson EO. *The ants*. Harvard University Press; Cambridge, Mass: 1990. p. 732.

Huelsenbeck JP, Ronquist F. MrBayes: Bayesian inference of phylogeny. *Bioinformatics*. 2001; 17:754–755.

Johnson C, Agosti D, Delabie JH, Dumpert K, Williams DJ, von Tschirnhaus M, Maschwitz U. *Acropyga* and *Azteca* ants (Hymenoptera: Formicidae) with scale insects (Sternorrhyncha: Coccoidea): 20 million years of intimate symbiosis. *American Museum Novitates*. 2001; 3335:1–18.

Kaufmann E, Malsch AKF, Williams DJ, Maschwitz U. *Pseudolasius* spp. (Formicinae) and their trophobionts - codispersal by colony budding. *Sociobiology*. 2003; 41:429–436.

Kjer KM, Blahnik RJ, Holzenthal R. Phylogeny of Trichoptera (Caddisflies): characterization of signal and noise within multiple datasets. *Systematic Biology*. 2001; 50:781–816.

Kjer KM. Use of rRNA secondary structure in phylogenetic studies to identify homologous positions: an example of alignment and data presentation from the frogs. *Molecular Phylogenetics and Evolution*. 1995; 4(3):314–330.

Klein RW, Kovac D, Schellerich A, Maschwitz U. Mealybug-carrying by swarming queens of a Southeast Asian bamboo-inhabiting ant. *Naturwissenschaften*. 1992; 79:422–423.

LaPolla JS, Cover SP, Mueller UG. Natural history of the mealybug-tending ant *Acropyga epedana*, with descriptions of the male and queen castes. *Transactions of the American Entomological Society*. 2002; 128(3):367–376.

LaPolla JS, Longino JT. An Unusual New *Brachymyrmex* Mayr (Hymenoptera: Formicidae) from Costa Rica, with Implications for the Phylogeny of the Lasiine Tribe Group. *Proceedings of the Washington Entomological Society*. 2006; 108(2):297–305.

LaPolla JS. *Acropyga* (Hymenoptera: Formicidae) of the World. Contributions of the American Entomological Institute. 2004; 33(3):1–130.

LaPolla JS. Ancient trophophoresy: A fossil *Acropyga* (Hymenoptera: Formicidae) from Dominican Amber. *Transactions of the American Entomological Society*. 2005; 131 (12):21–28.

Lutzoni F, Wagner P, Reeb V, Zoller S. Integrating ambiguously aligned regions of DNA sequences in phylogenetic analyses without violating positional homology. *Systematic Biology*. 2000; 49:628–651.

Malsch AKF, Kaufmann E, Heckroth HP, Williams DJ, Maryati M, Maschwitz U. Continuous transfer of subterranean mealybugs (Hemiptera, Pseudococcidae) by *Pseudolasius* spp. (Hymenoptera, Formicidae) during colony fission. *Insectes Sociaux*. 2001; 48(4):333–341.

Mueller UG, Rehner SA, Schultz TR. The evolution of agriculture in ants. *Science*. 1998; 281:2034–2038.

Posada D, Crandall KA. Modeltest: testing the model of DNA substitution. *Bioinformatics*. 1998; 14:817–818.

Sallum MAM, Schultz TR, Foster PG, Aronstein K, Wirtz RA, Wilkerson RC. Phylogeny of Anophelinae (Diptera: Culicidae) based on nuclear ribosomal and mitochondrial DNA sequences. *Systematic Entomology*. 2002; 27:361–382.

Schultz TR, Mueller UG, Currie CR, Rehner SA. Fernando Vega and Meredith: Ecological and Evolutionary Advances in Insect-Fungal Associations. Oxford University Press; New York: 2005. Reciprocal illumination:A comparison of agriculture in humans and ants; pp. 149–190.

Shattuck SO. Higher classification of the ant subfamilies Aneuretinae, Dolichoderinae, and Formicinae (Hymenoptera: Formicidae) *Systematic Entomology*. 1992; 17:199–206.

Snelling RR. *Aphomomyrmex* and a related new genus of arboreal African ants. Contributions in Science. 1979; 316:1–8.

Swofford DL. PAUP*. *Phylogenetic Analysis Using Parsimony* (*and Other Methods) Version 4. Sinauer Associates; Sunderland, Massachusetts: 2002.

Villesen P, Mueller UG, Schultz TR, Adams RMM, Bouck MC. Evolution of ant-cultivar specialization and cultivar switching in *Apterostigma* fungus-growing ants. *Evolution*. 2004; 58:2252–2265.

Ward PS, Brady SG. Phylogeny and biogeography of the ant subfamily Myrmeciinae (Hymenoptera: Formicidae) Invertebrate Systematics. 2003; 17:361–386.

Ward PS. Taxonomy, phylogeny, and biogeography of the ant genus *Tetraponera* (Hymenoptera: Formicidae) in the Oriental and Australian regions. *Invertebrate Taxonomy*. 2001; 15:589–665.

Way MJ. Mutualism between ants and honeydew-producing Homoptera. *Annual Review of Entomology*. 1963; 8:307–344.

Index